D0454630

NATIONAL
AUDUBON
SOCIETY

FIRST
FIELD
GUIDE

WEATHER

Scholastic Inc.
New York   Toronto   London   Auckland   Sydney

NATIONAL AUDUBON SOCIETY

FIRST FIELD GUIDE

WEATHER

Written by
Jonathan D. W. Kahl

The National Audubon Society, established in 1905, has 550,000 members and more than 500 chapters nationwide. Its mission is to conserve and restore natural ecosystems, focusing on nature and wildlife, and these guides are part of that mission. Celebrating the beauty and wonders of nature, Audubon looks toward its second century of educating people of all ages. For information about Audubon membership, contact:

National Audubon Society
700 Broadway
New York, NY 10003-9562
212-979-3000   800-274-4201
http://www.audubon.org

Dedicated to the living memory of Dr. Howard H. Rye

LIBRARY OF CONGRESS CATALOGING-IN-PUBLICATION DATA
Kahl, Jonathan D.
    National Audubon Society first field guide to weather / Jonathan
Kahl.
        p.   cm.
    Summary: Provides an overview of various weather conditions, how
they develop, and how they are studied.
    Includes index.
    ISBN 0-590-05469-4 (hc). — ISBN 0-590-05488-0 (pb)
    1. Meteorology—Juvenile lieterature.   2. Weather—Obesrvers'
manuals—Juvenile literature.   [1. Weather.   2. Meteorology.]
I. Title.
QC863.5.K29   1998
551.5—dc21   98-2938

ISBN 0-590-05469-4 (HC)
ISBN 0-590-05488-0 (PB)

10 9 8 7 6 5 4 3 2 1   8   9/9   0/0   01   02   03

Printed in Hong Kong
First printing, September 1998

Contents

What is weather?

How to look at weather

Field guide

Reference

About this book

Whether you are weather watching while sitting in your own backyard, while hiking in the mountains, or while on vacation at the beach, this book will help you look at weather the way a meteorologist does. The book is divided into four parts:

Lightning page 92

PART 1: What is weather?

tells you about weather, climate, the atmosphere, the sun, the seasons, and other things that you need to know about so that you can understand the weather.

PART 2: How to look at weather

gives you the information you need to begin identifying the different types of clouds, storms, and other things you see in the sky; tells you how to build your own weather instruments; and gives you tips for forecasting the weather.

PART 3: The field guide includes detailed descriptions, season and range information, and dramatic photographs of 50 kinds of clouds, storms, and other weather-related things you might see.

PART 4: The reference section at the back of the book includes a helpful glossary of terms used by meteorologists; lists of useful books, videos, CDs, Web sites, and organizations; and an index of the clouds, weather systems, and other weather events covered in the field guide.

What is a meteorologist?

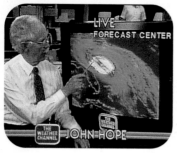

A meteorologist is a scientist who studies and predicts the weather. Meteorologists use sophisticated equipment, like Doppler radar and supercomputers, but they also rely on old-fashioned sky watching.

America's first meteorologist

Benjamin Franklin (1706–1790) was one of the first meteorologists. In 1752, he conducted his famous kite-flying experiment, in which he flew a metal-tipped kite during a thunderstorm and observed how a spark from a lightning

Benjamin Franklin conducting his kite-flying experiment

bolt traveled from the kite down its string and onto an attached metal key. When he touched the key, he got an electrical shock. Franklin's experiment proved that lightning is a giant spark of electricity. Do not do this yourself! Many people who have tried to copy Franklin's experiment have been killed.

WHEN LIGHTNING STRIKES

Franklin also invented the lightning rod, which is still used all over the world to protect buildings and ships from lightning strikes. The rod is made of metal, so lightning strikes the rod instead of the structure it is attached to.

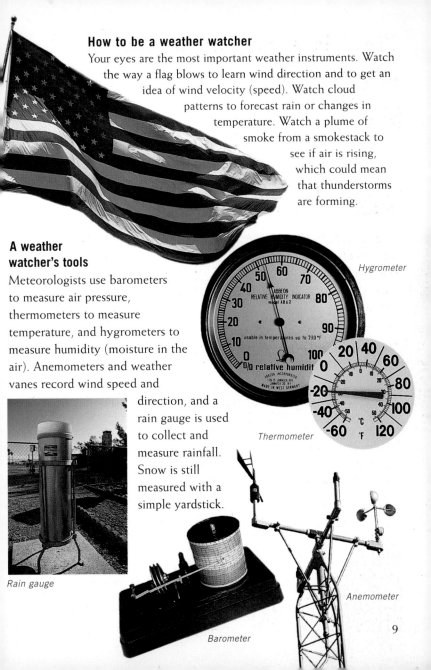

How to be a weather watcher

Your eyes are the most important weather instruments. Watch the way a flag blows to learn wind direction and to get an idea of wind velocity (speed). Watch cloud patterns to forecast rain or changes in temperature. Watch a plume of smoke from a smokestack to see if air is rising, which could mean that thunderstorms are forming.

A weather watcher's tools

Meteorologists use barometers to measure air pressure, thermometers to measure temperature, and hygrometers to measure humidity (moisture in the air). Anemometers and weather vanes record wind speed and direction, and a rain gauge is used to collect and measure rainfall. Snow is still measured with a simple yardstick.

Hygrometer

Thermometer

Rain gauge

Anemometer

Barometer

9

What is weather?

Weather describes the condition of the air at a particular place and time. Weather also tells how air moves (wind) and describes anything it might be carrying, such as rain, snow, or clouds. Thunder, lightning, rainbows, haze, and other special events are all part of weather.

Weather and climate

Climate is the word used to describe the average weather conditions in a certain place or during a certain season. Weather may change from day to day, but climate changes only over hundreds or thousands of years. Many animals and plants need one kind of climate to survive. Manatees and palm trees can live only in a warm climate, while Caribou and spruce trees need a cold climate.

Volcanoes National Park, Hawaii

An Arizona desert

WET AND DRY

Dry climates, such as in the deserts of southern Arizona and New Mexico, are hot and have little rainfall. Tropical climates, like those in southern Florida and Hawaii, are warm, humid, and rainy.

ON THE MOVE

Many species of birds and whales and even some butterflies migrate, which means that they travel long distances as the seasons change to find the climates they prefer. The background photograph shows migrating Snow Geese.

Good and bad

Weather affects many things in our lives, from the clothes we wear to the foods we eat. Farmers choose, plant, and harvest their crops depending on the weather. The right kind of weather lets us enjoy special activities, such as picnics on sunny days or skiing on snowy days.

Skiers in Eldora, Colorado

Storm clouds over Wind Cave National Park, South Dakota

Bad weather can mean slippery sidewalks, canceled soccer games, or even school closings. Tornadoes, droughts, floods, and other extreme weather can damage homes and even kill people.

The atmosphere

The atmosphere surrounding the earth is made up of many protective layers of air. Air is mostly a mixture of nitrogen, oxygen, and other gases, but it also has floating solid and liquid particles, mainly in the form of clouds, sea salt, dust, and smoke.

Water vapor is a gas in the atmosphere. There is very little of it in the air—water vapor is only 1 to 4 percent of the atmosphere—but without it we would have no clouds, rain, or snow. Water vapor is one of the greenhouse gases, which help to trap the earth's heat; carbon dioxide is another.

Light as air?

The weight of the air pressing down on the earth is called air pressure. Over 2,000 pounds (900 kg) of air presses down on every square foot of the earth's surface. Air pressure can change from place to place, and this causes air to move, flowing from areas of high (heavier) pressure toward areas of low (lighter) pressure. On high mountain peaks, the air is very thin, and its low pressure does not contain enough oxygen for breathing.

Layers of the atmosphere

The troposphere is the bottom layer of the earth's atmosphere. It rises 6 to 12 miles (10–20 km) from the ground. It is thinner near the north and south poles and thicker near the equator. *Tropos* is a Greek word meaning "change," and most of the earth's changeable weather—like clouds, storms, rain, and snow—occurs in the troposphere. Next comes the stratosphere, where the ozone layer filters out most of the sun's dangerous ultraviolet rays. Above the stratosphere are the mesosphere, thermosphere, and exosphere. These layers have little to do with weather but they have other important jobs. For example, the thermosphere burns up millions of meteors that strike the earth's atmosphere each day.

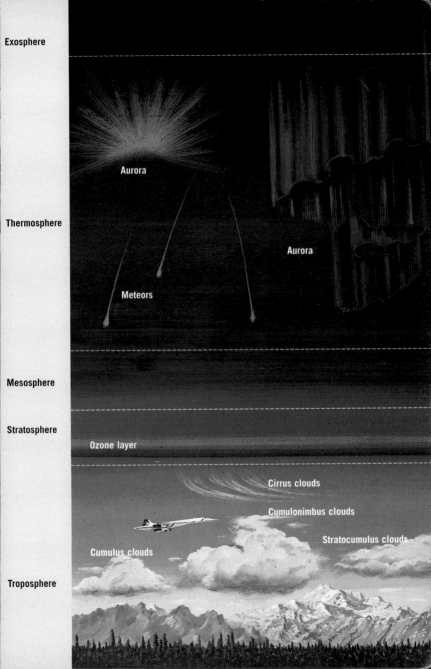

Exosphere

Thermosphere

Aurora

Aurora

Meteors

Mesosphere

Stratosphere

Ozone layer

Cirrus clouds

Cumulonimbus clouds

Stratocumulus clouds

Cumulus clouds

Troposphere

The sun

The sun is responsible for most of the earth's weather, even though it is 93 million miles (150 million km) away. Its intense heat gives energy to the earth's atmosphere and sets it in motion.

Natural nuclear energy

The sun is a star, 868,000 miles (1.4 million km) across, in the center of our solar system. The temperature at the sun's core is a whopping 27 million degrees Fahrenheit (15 million degrees Centigrade), but at the surface it is a mere 10,000°F (5,500°C). The sun energizes all nine planets in the solar system.

The speed of light

The energy the sun gives off is called electromagnetic radiation. Energy often moves in waves, like ocean waves or ripples in a pond. Traveling at the speed of light, 186,000 miles (300,000 km) per second, the sun's energy moves through space in invisible waves of different lengths.

V I S I B L E   L I G H T

◄ ULTRAVIOLET

INFRARED ►

The shortest of the sun's energy waves are called ultraviolet radiation. Slightly longer waves are called visible light. Different lengths of visible light waves give us light of different colors. Still longer waves are called infrared radiation. Other kinds of waves given off by the sun include X rays, microwaves, TV waves, and radio waves.

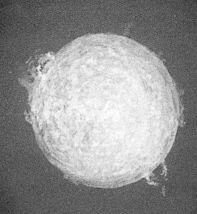

HOT AND COLD

Mercury (on the left in the background photograph), the planet closest to the sun (on the right), has temperatures up to 800°F (420°C). Pluto, the planet farthest from the sun, is thought to have temperatures as low as −375°F (−224°C). Our planet Earth, third closest to the sun, has an average temperature of 59°F (15°C), but temperatures as hot as 136°F (57°C) and as cold as −127°F (−87°C) have been recorded.

The glass roof of a greenhouse recycles the sun's heat energy in much the same way that the earth's atmosphere does.

Recycle that heat!

The sun's energy warms up the land and the oceans at the earth's surface. Dark surfaces like blue water and green forests absorb the most heat. Bright surfaces like ice, snow, and clouds act like mirrors and reflect heat. As the earth warms, it also gives off heat. The atmosphere—the layers of air surrounding the earth—is a giant "recycling machine" for heat, letting most of the sun's energy pass through but trapping a portion of the earth's energy from escaping out into space. This is called the greenhouse effect.

15

The seasons

Why does the weather change at the same times each year? Because the earth's position in relation to the sun is always changing.

Day and night

The earth spins around its axis, an imaginary line that runs between the north and south poles. One complete spin takes 24 hours, and at any moment, half of the earth is lighted and warmed by the sun (day), while the other half faces away from the sun (night). While it spins, the earth also moves around the sun in a circle, called an orbit, which takes one year to complete.

Spring equinox,
March 21

Summer solstice,
June 21

day

night

Fall equinox,
September 21

A tilted world

As the earth moves and spins, it is tilted in one direction at an angle of 23 degrees, like the minute hand on a clock when it is four minutes after the hour. It stays tilted all the time as it orbits the sun, so that each area of earth receives different amounts of the sun's energy at different times of the year. This is why we have seasons.

LAND OF THE MIDNIGHT SUN

Near the north and south poles, winter and summer last six months each. In summer, the sun shines 24 hours a day, but winter days are completely dark. This photograph shows the sun's position over a five-hour period in July in northern Alaska. Notice how the sun never sets below the horizon.

A summer night in Alaska

Winter solstice, December 21

Hot and cold

In December, the earth's Northern Hemisphere is tilted away from the sun and gets less of the sun's energy. The temperature is cold, the days are short, and the nights are long. The shortest day and the longest night of the year is called the winter solstice. In June, when the summer solstice occurs, the Northern Hemisphere has its longest day and shortest night. On the spring and fall equinoxes, day and night are about equal (12 hours long).

Summer, Grand Tetons, Wyoming

WARM AND COOL

The difference between summer and winter weather conditions is greatest in the Northern Hemisphere. This is because land warms and cools more rapidly than water, and there are more land masses in the Northern Hemisphere.

17

Winter, Grand Tetons, Wyoming

Moisture in the air

Water is a peculiar substance. Depending on its temperature, it can be a solid (ice or snow), a liquid (water), or a gas (water vapor). In fact, water has a "triple point" temperature, 32°F (0°C), at

There is always water in the air— sometimes you can see it!

which it can exist in all three forms together! Water vapor, or moisture, is one of the most important features of weather.

ANOTHER RECYCLING MACHINE

Water is constantly moving between the oceans, the land, and the air. It rises (evaporates) from the oceans, lakes, and rivers to form clouds. It falls from the clouds (precipitates) and seeps into the ground. It flows into streams, rivers, and lakes, which eventually lead back to the oceans. This process is known as the water cycle.

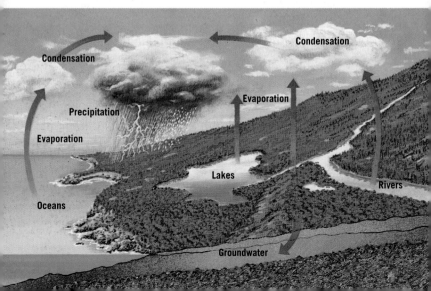

Condensation

Condensation

Evaporation

Precipitation

Evaporation

Lakes

Rivers

Oceans

Groundwater

Invisible water

Water vapor is an invisible gas in the air. The amount of water vapor, which is called the relative humidity, can be anywhere between 0 and 100 percent. A relative humidity of 100 percent means that the air is saturated—as full of water vapor as it can be. Most

Fog is a cloud that forms near the ground when air with lots of water vapor in it cools.

water vapor comes from evaporation. When the sun heats the liquid water in the earth's oceans, lakes, and rivers, some of it changes into water vapor and rises into the air. The atmosphere also gets small amounts of water vapor from plants and from moisture in soil.

Water condenses on a window when warm air inside cools against the colder glass.

The dew point

The temperature at which condensation occurs is called the dew point. If the air is moist, it does not need to cool very much to reach the point of condensation. If the air is dry, then the air must cool a lot before condensation occurs.

Where do clouds come from?

Warm air can hold more water vapor than cold air. When air cools to a temperature too low to hold all of its water vapor, some of the water vapor changes back into liquid water. This process is called condensation. Condensation is important to weather because it is the way that clouds form.

A spider's web covered with morning dew

What is a cloud?

Clouds are floating collections of tiny water droplets or, at colder temperatures, ice crystals. Sometimes they are a mixture of both water and ice. Individual cloud droplets are so

A mixture of different cloud types page 84

small that it takes about a million of them to form just one raindrop! Clouds come in many different sizes and shapes, from puffy cotton-ball cumulus to thunderstorm clouds 6 miles (10 km) tall. Clouds can form at ground level, at great heights in the atmosphere, and everywhere in between. They can evaporate, precipitate (drop rain or snow), or produce destructive tornadoes. Clouds offer important clues to understanding and forecasting the weather.

Look out below!

Why don't clouds fall from the sky? They do! Clouds are made of liquid water or ice, both of which are heavier than air. But while gravity pulls the cloud droplets and ice crystals down, air pressure pushes them back up. Because of this pulling

Mountain cloud page 78

and pushing, they fall very slowly and usually evaporate long before they reach the earth.

Odd-shaped lenticular cloud (page 79), with altocumulus clouds (page 58) in the background

How do clouds form?

Clouds start to form when air cools and the water vapor condenses into tiny liquid droplets. The droplets form around microscopic particles floating in the air. These particles, called condensation nuclei, can be anything: tiny specks of windblown soil, salt from ocean spray, grains of pollen from flowers, or even bacteria. There are lots of condensation nuclei floating around—at least 10,000 can be found in the small volume of air that would fill a thimble! If it is cold enough, the droplets can turn into ice.

ICE CLOUDS OR WATER CLOUDS?

It is easy to tell whether clouds are made of ice or water. Water clouds have sharp edges, making it easy to see where the cloud stops, while ice clouds have fuzzy edges. Knowing whether a cloud is made of ice or water gives us an idea of the temperature at the cloud's altitude.

Ice clouds

Water clouds

21

Where the clouds are

Different cloud types form from the different ways that water vapor cools and changes into water or ice. Different clouds form at different altitudes (heights) in the sky. The drawing on this page shows where different types of clouds form in the sky and what they typically look like.

Altocumulus
page 58

Altostratus
page 60

Cumulonimbus
page 70

Stratocumulus
page 64

Cumulus
page 68

Nimbostratus
page 63

Stratus
page 62

Fog
page 66

NAMING THE CLOUDS

In 1803, the British scientist Luke Howard named the clouds using Latin words that described their characteristics. Howard's cloud classification system is still in use today. Delicate high-altitude ice clouds are called cirrus, which means "lock of hair" in Latin. Puffy cumulus clouds are named after the word for "heap." The flat clouds that sometimes cover the entire sky are called stratus, which means "layer." Precipitating clouds—clouds that rain or snow—always have some form of the word nimbus, meaning "rain," in their names.

Cirrus
page 50

Cirrocumulus
page 52

Cirrostratus
page 54

Contrails
page 56

WHAT'S IN A NAME?

Prefixes (the beginning of a cloud's name) indicate a cloud's altitude. Middle clouds, which are one to three miles (1½–5 km) high, have the prefix "alto," while high clouds above three miles (5 km) have the prefix "cirro." Low clouds have no prefix.

Precipitation

Nearly four-fifths of the earth is covered by water. Water evaporates from the oceans, lakes, and rivers; it rises and condenses into clouds; then it falls back to the earth as precipitation.

A rainy day in New York City

Precipitation can be any type of water falling from the sky, including rain, sleet, hail, or snow.

How do raindrops form?

Cloud droplets grow larger by bumping into one another and sticking together, a process meteorologists call collision and coalescence. It takes a million cloud droplets to make just one raindrop, so millions of collisions must take place inside a rain-producing cloud. Collisions are caused by the moving air inside clouds. Also, larger droplets fall faster than smaller ones and can swallow up small drops beneath them as they fall.

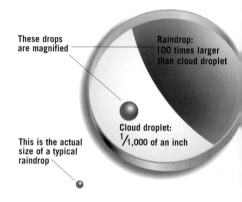

These drops are magnified

Raindrop: 100 times larger than cloud droplet

Cloud droplet: 1/1,000 of an inch

This is the actual size of a typical raindrop

TOO SMALL TO FALL?

Ordinary cloud droplets measure less than one one-thousandth of an inch wide. Because they are so tiny and light, they fall very slowly, sometimes taking an hour to fall only 100 feet (30 m)! They evaporate long before reaching the ground. Raindrops, however, are over 100 times larger and fall at speeds of up to 20 miles (30 km) per hour.

Millions of snowflakes

Snowflakes come in millions of different shapes. Inside a cloud, most ice crystals are shaped like plates, columns, or branches. Beneath the cloud the falling crystals smash into each other, partially melt, refreeze, and smash again and again on their way toward the ground. Snowflakes falling on the ground contain fragments of thousands of different shattered and melted ice crystals. Is it any wonder that no two are the same?

Snow in summer?

Even on warm summer days, the temperature high up in the atmosphere can be below freezing. The tops of tall thunderstorm clouds contain both ice crystals and supercooled water droplets (liquid water that exists at below-freezing temperatures). The ice crystals grow very quickly as the droplets evaporate. When these large heavy crystals fall through the lower, warmer part of the cloud, they melt into raindrops. This means that most of our warm-season rain starts out as snow!

Snow that forms in warmer temperatures is softer, with ice crystals that stick together—this is a good type of snow for sculpting.

Thunderstorms: a big bang

A thunderstorm is one of the most dramatic weather events. With the right ingredients—rising air and plenty of moisture—a small puffy cumulus cloud can grow into a towering, anvil-shaped thunderstorm cloud in as little as half an hour! All thunderstorms produce lightning—an enormous and very hot spark of electricity. Thunder is the explosive sound of air expanding as it is heated by lightning. Severe thunderstorms can produce strong winds, large hail, heavy downpours, and even tornadoes.

How thunderstorms grow

A thunderstorm starts with a cumulus cloud that forms as moisture condenses in fast-rising air, called an updraft. The cumulus cloud grows taller and taller, usually very quickly, until it produces rain, lightning, thunder, and sometimes hail. As the rain continues, the thunderstorm cloud loses its water. Eventually the rain stops and the cloud evaporates, often leaving only high cirrus clouds to remind us of the storm.

This series of four photographs shows the growth of a cumulus cloud into a thunderstorm.

What is lightning?

Lightning is a giant electrical spark. As the water droplets and ice crystals slosh around inside a thunderstorm cloud's strong updrafts and downdrafts, electrical charges are generated. When the electrical charges become very large, electricity is released in a bolt of lightning.

Lightning bolts heat up the air to an amazing 54,000°F (30,000°C). That's more than five times hotter than the surface of the sun!

Lightning can be deadly, so stay inside during thunderstorms. Keep away from metal, such as faucets and pipes, and do not use the telephone. If you are outside, stay away from water (this means no swimming!). If possible, take shelter in a car with a metal roof. If no shelter is available, crouch down on both feet in a low dry area.

Lightning over Tucson, Arizona

Twisting tornadoes

Tornadoes begin as funnel clouds—spinning columns of air (called vortexes) that drop down from severe thunderstorms. When they reach the ground they become tornadoes. Tornadoes are between 300 and 2,000 feet (90–600 m) wide and travel at speeds of 20 to 45 miles (30–70 km) per hour. They usually last only a few minutes, but their spinning winds, up to 300 miles (480 km) per hour, can lift houses into the air.

RATING A TORNADO

Professor T. Fujita developed a scale for classifying tornadoes based on wind speed and destructive power. F1 tornadoes can break windows and snap small trees. F5 tornadoes can flatten steel and concrete buildings.

A developing tornado, Texas

Tornado Alley

Tornado Alley, which stretches from Texas to Iowa, is home to most of the world's tornadoes. From March through July, these states are a battleground for cold dry Canadian air that collides with warm moist tropical air from the Gulf of Mexico.

If tornadoes threaten your area, keep a battery-powered radio handy so you can listen to the watches and warnings issued by the National Weather Service. If a tornado is present, seek shelter in a basement or the deepest interior of a strong building, and keep clear of windows. If you are caught outside, do not try to outrun a tornado. If you are in a car, get out and lie flat in a low-lying area or ditch.

Hurricanes: tropical disasters

Hurricanes are the planet's most destructive storms. They are intense cyclones with swirling winds up to 150 miles (240 km) per hour. Usually around 300 miles (480 km) across, hurricanes are 1,000 to 5,000 times larger than tornadoes! Hurricanes are known by different names around the world. In Japan they are called typhoons, while Australians call them willy-willys.

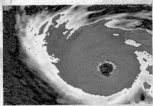
Satellite image of Hurricane Diana over U.S. east coast, September 1984

How hurricanes form

Hurricanes form over warm tropical oceans, where evaporating water makes the air quite humid. Warm air rises because it is lighter than cool air. As the tropical air rises and condenses, huge amounts of heat are released into the air.

RATING A HURRICANE

The Saffir-Simpson Hurricane Intensity Scale describes the damage hurricanes can cause to coastal areas. Category 1 storms are moderately destructive, while Category 5 storms cause massive damage and require people to leave the area before they hit.

People in hurricane-prone areas should keep battery-powered radios handy and listen for the National Weather Service's hurricane watches and warnings, issued when a hurricane is expected to strike an area within 24 hours. Local authorities may instruct residents to board up windows or even evacuate their homes.

The east coast of the United States frequently gets slammed by hurricanes traveling north from the Caribbean Sea. When hurricanes reach land, where there is less water to evaporate, they lose their energy and die out.

Damage from Hurricane Andrew, Florida, August 1992

Wind: air in motion

Air is fluid. Like ocean currents, the atmosphere flows in many directions. These flows, called wind, spread the sun's heat energy over the planet and create different weather patterns. Wind is invisible, of course, but its effects are easy to observe. We can watch clouds, plumes of smoke, or flags to get an idea of wind speed and direction.

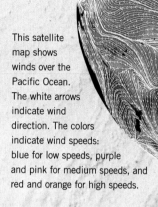

This satellite map shows winds over the Pacific Ocean. The white arrows indicate wind direction. The colors indicate wind speeds: blue for low speeds, purple and pink for medium speeds, and red and orange for high speeds.

Watch a smokestack to observe turbulence. Loopy twisting plumes tell you the air is turbulent; flat plumes indicate little turbulence.

A roller coaster of air

The earth is bumpy. Air pushes and rubs against mountains, trees, buildings, and even ocean waves as the wind moves it around. This rubbing, called friction, slows the wind down. Where the land is smooth or over water, there is less friction and winds are stronger. Wind is rarely steady. It moves in gusts and lulls. These irregularities in the wind are called turbulence. Lots of things can cause turbulence, including air rubbing against bumpy ground, or fast-rising air inside thunderstorm clouds.

What causes wind?

Different forces work together to cause wind.

Pressure gradient force. When you pop a balloon, the air inside it rushes out. This happens because there are different air pressures inside and outside the balloon. On the earth, sunlight causes different areas to have different air pressures. The pressure differences, called gradients, cause the air to start moving in the same way that popping a balloon does.

Coriolis force. The spinning of the earth changes the direction of the wind. As the wind blows, the earth spins beneath the moving air, causing winds to curve. The Coriolis force, first discovered in 1835 by the French scientist Gustave-Gaspard de Coriolis, causes Northern Hemisphere winds to curve to the right and Southern Hemisphere winds to curve to the left.

Wind direction is described as the direction the air is moving *from*. A northeast wind blows from the northeast toward the southwest.

Sailboat on stormy seas

Palm trees bending in hurricane winds

Wind systems

Wind patterns come in all sizes. There are giant wind belts that circle the globe and affect weather all over the world. There are also smaller local systems.

Wind belts

Trade winds. The trade winds are the two wind belts located north and south of the equator. Because they are steady east winds, the trades provided a dependable ocean route for trading ships sailing westward from Europe to the Americas. The two belts collide near the equator in an area of cloudy, rainy weather called the intertropical convergence zone. This is where many of the world's thunderstorms develop.

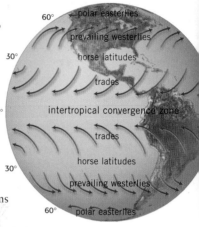

Doldrums. The doldrums, an area of light winds and calm weather, are also found near the equator.

Horse latitudes. The horse latitudes are two weak wind belts north and south of the trades. Sailing ships used to get stranded here because there was not enough wind to propel them. To lighten their load and save water, sailors sometimes threw their animals (including horses) overboard.

Prevailing westerlies. The prevailing westerlies are large wind belts that blow from the west. They cause major weather patterns, such as high- and low-pressure systems, to travel from west to east across the United States.

Polar easterlies. The polar easterlies are the wind belts closest to the north and south poles. The polar winds usually blow from the east, but intense storms called polar lows sometimes form over the polar oceans, causing winds to blow in a circle much like hurricane winds.

The Asian monsoon brings over 400 inches (1,000 cm) of summer rain to parts of India as warm humid air blows in off the Bay of Bengal.

Local wind systems

There are many smaller wind systems that influence local weather. Monsoons are wind systems in many parts of the world that can change directions in different seasons. Mountain-valley breezes and sea breezes are local winds that can change their direction every day. Downslope winds, such as Colorado's chinook and Switzerland's foehn, blow down mountainsides and bring fast-moving warm air that quickly melts the snow cover. Chinook is a Native American word that means "snow eater."

RIVERS IN THE AIR

Jet streams are narrow currents of air located very high up (about 30,000 feet, 9,000 m) in the atmosphere. They travel at extremely high speeds, often moving faster than 100 miles (160 km) per hour. Jet streams snake around the globe in great loops to the north and south and help to form the high- and low-pressure systems that control weather.

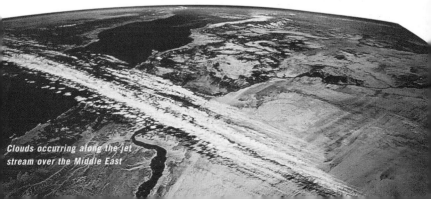

Clouds occurring along the jet stream over the Middle East

Pressure systems

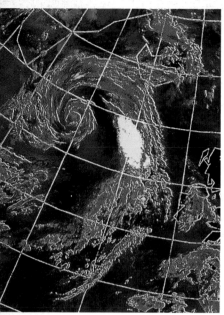

This satellite image shows a low-pressure system over the North Atlantic Ocean. Yellow and red indicate low-altitude clouds, while white indicates high-altitude clouds.

High- and low-pressure systems are huge masses of spinning air, often more than 1,000 miles (1,600 km) across. The spinning is created as high-altitude air flows around peaks and dips in the wavy jet stream. In the Northern Hemisphere, highs spin in a clockwise direction and lows spin counterclockwise. As air inside high- and low-pressure systems spins, it also spirals toward the area of lowest pressure.

Watching the barometer

The barometer, which measures air pressure, is a favorite instrument of both meteorologists and amateur weather watchers. The rising and falling air pressures reported by the barometer are closely associated with changing weather conditions. Each type of pressure system comes with distinct weather patterns.

High-pressure systems typically bring bright blue skies.

High-pressure weather

In a high-pressure system, the lowest air pressure is located outside the air mass, so the air spirals outward. This creates an empty space in the high's center, which is filled in by air coming down from higher altitudes. Highs typically bring clear skies and pleasant weather. Clear skies are not always a blessing, though. Cold waves—surges of frigid Arctic air into the United States—occur during wintertime high-pressure systems. In summer, highs with very slow-moving winds allow air pollution to build up to unhealthy levels.

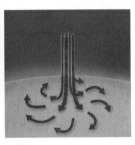

HIGH-PRESSURE SYSTEM
Air under high pressure sinks, leaving clear skies. In these drawings the arrows show the movement of the air.

Low-pressure weather

In a low-pressure system the lowest air pressure is located in the center, so the air spins inward. This movement creates a pileup of air in the center of the spinning air mass. The air in the center has nowhere to go but up, so it rises, cools, and condenses, creating clouds. Lows usually mean bad weather. In winter, lows sometimes deliver heavy snowfalls or ice storms. In warmer months, lows can mean thunderstorms and severe weather.

LOW-PRESSURE SYSTEM
Air under low pressure rises and cools, forming clouds and sometimes precipitation.

35

Air masses and fronts

Shortly after World War I a group of Norwegian meteorologists noticed that most weather activity occurs in long narrow bands of contrasting temperatures. Borrowing a military term, they called these battlegrounds of cold and warm air "fronts."

Air moves around in giant chunks called air masses. Each air mass has its own levels of temperature and humidity. Because of its size, often 1,000 miles (1,600 km) wide, an air mass can take several days to pass over an area. When two air masses bump into each other, they create a boundary called a front. There are several kinds of fronts.

Stationary front

A stationary front is the boundary between side-by-side cold and warm air masses. Typical stationary-front weather includes cloudy skies and light rain or snow. When the air masses begin to collide with each other, warm and cold fronts are born.

COLD FRONT

Cumulonimbus clouds

Nimbostratus clouds

Cold air

Warm air

Cold front

When a cold air mass bumps into a warm air mass, a cold front is created. Because cold air is heavier than warm air, the cold air wedges underneath the retreating warm air and forces it upward at a steep angle. The swiftly rising air quickly cools, forming clouds and heavy precipitation. Cold fronts are often associated with thunderstorms.

A halo around the sun often appears in advance of a warm front.

Warm front

A warm front forms when a warm air mass collides with a cold air mass. Warm air is lighter than cold air, so it glides upward as it pushes the cold air mass aside. The gentle upward movement causes slower precipitation.

Occluded front

Cold fronts sometimes catch up to and overtake warm fronts, lifting them higher into the air. The result is an occluded front, and it brings a combination of cold-front weather and warm-front weather.

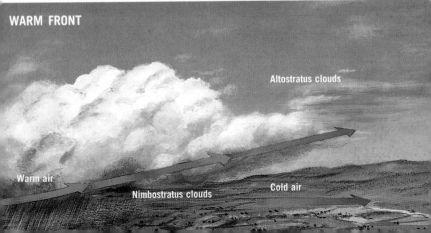

WARM FRONT

Altostratus clouds

Warm air

Nimbostratus clouds

Cold air

Weather forecasting

Weather forecasting has dramatically improved in recent years because of faster supercomputers, better satellites and radar, and a clearer understanding of how weather works.

This satellite image of North and South America shows low-altitude clouds in yellow, high-altitude clouds in white, and land in green and orange.

Weather scientists

Meteorologists prepare their forecasts in two stages. First, they study current weather conditions by examining weather maps, radar and satellite images, and local weather measurements. Next, they use their knowledge of meteorology to predict how the current conditions will change.

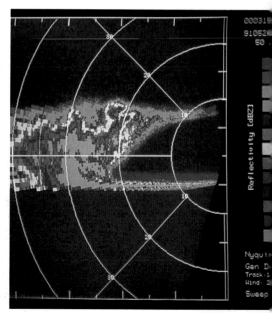

Doppler radar screen

Modern weather stations

Automatic weather stations are powered by the sun's energy. They record local weather conditions and use communications satellites to send those measurements to forecasting centers. These modern stations make it possible to get weather information from faraway and hard-to-reach places, such as mountaintops or polar regions.

Meteorologist at the National Severe Storm Laboratory, Oklahoma

Doppler radar tower

A Radiosonde launch

Windows to the sky

Radiosondes are miniature weather stations carried by gas-filled balloons. They float as high as 20 miles (30 km) in the sky. Thousands of these stations are released every 12 hours at locations around the world. They give us important information about winds, temperatures, and humidity in the upper atmosphere.

Improving accuracy

Weather forecasting will never be 100 percent accurate. The atmosphere, with all its clouds, wind systems, storms, fronts, and spinning air patterns, is impossible to predict perfectly. Forecasts will continue to improve, however, as we build faster computers and find better ways to measure the atmosphere.

Weather forecasting computers

Maps, satellites, and radar

Weather maps make sense of the thousands of weather measurements available every hour of every day. Instead of looking at pages and pages of numbers, meteorologists can study the lines, symbols, and colors on a map to understand

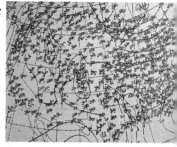

Detailed weather map

complicated weather patterns at a glance and to predict how they will change over time. Weather maps can show both general large-scale weather patterns and local weather conditions.

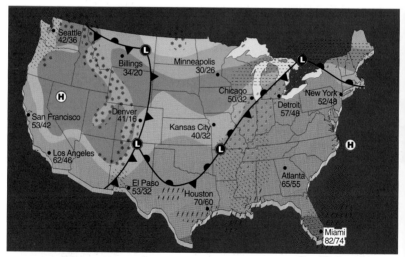

Simplified weather map

Television and newspaper weather maps

Many television stations and newspapers prepare simplified weather maps for the general public. These maps are usually colorful descriptions of weather patterns that show temperatures, clouds, and areas of precipitation.

Satellite images

Weather instruments on space satellites can view the sky from far above the earth. Two common types of satellite images are taken in visible and infrared wavelengths. In visible-wavelength images, white areas indicate where clouds are present. Infrared images show cloud temperatures. The satellites can take images quickly, one after another. Computer programs use these consecutive satellite images to analyze how cloud patterns move with the winds.

In this infrared satellite image, blue indicates colder areas and red indicates warmer areas.

In this visible-wavelength satellite image, the dark area on the lower left side shows the moon's shadow during the solar eclipse of July 11, 1991.

Doppler radar

Radar, which has been used in weather forecasting for decades, sends out radio waves that bounce off water droplets and ice crystals. Doppler radar is an advanced kind of radar that measures wind speed and finds areas of precipitation. Doppler radar can show the location and intensity of precipitation and can also detect thunderstorms and tornadoes.

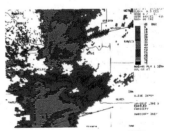

The red area near the center of this Doppler radar image is a thunderstorm.

Using and changing the weather

Weather is a powerful force of nature. With 6,000 trillion tons of air in constant motion, the atmosphere provides an enormous source of energy. As mighty as the atmosphere is, though, we still have the power to change it. Some people try to make rain by dropping chemicals into the clouds. Other changes, such as the thinning of the ozone layer, are accidental.

Cloud seeding with rockets, Colorado

Cloud farming

Since the 1940s, meteorologists have been trying to make rain by dropping tiny silver-iodide crystals into clouds. These particles serve as condensation nuclei, the "seeds" around which ice crystals grow. Some scientists believe that cloud seeding can increase the amount of precipitation that falls from rain clouds. Others believe it is impossible to know how much rain might have fallen anyway, even if the cloud had not been seeded.

Weather energy

Sun and wind can be captured to supply pollution-free energy for the earth's population. Solar energy is popular in hot dry regions, such as the Middle East, the southwestern United States, and parts of Australia. Many people use solar power to heat water in their homes.

Solar mirrors, California

Wind generators produce electricity in many parts of the world. There are nearly 20,000 wind turbines (giant windmills) in California alone.

Turbine and windmill, California

Beware of the sun!

High up in the stratosphere, the ozone layer is thinning. This thinning is taking place in many areas, but mainly over Antarctica, where cold temperatures and strange chemicals like CFCs (chlorofluorocarbons) break down the ozone gas. Because of this thinning ozone layer, more and more of the sun's harmful ultraviolet rays are reaching the earth's surface. Beachgoers everywhere should use sunscreen to protect their skin from these harmful cancer-causing rays. Governments around the world recognize the problem of CFCs and are taking steps to avoid releasing them into the atmosphere.

Waikiki Beach, Hawaii

Watching the weather

Remember, your eyes are the most important weather instrument. Be observant! Keep track of your observations. Soon you will be making your own weather predictions.

KEEP A WEATHER NOTEBOOK

Good record keeping will help you learn the kinds of weather that are associated with different cloud patterns, wind shifts, and other sky phenomena. Record your observations every day to better understand the changing weather patterns.

LOCAL WEATHER MAPS

One of the best ways to make your own forecast is to locate the highs and lows on a local newspaper or television weather map. Which kind of pressure system is near your location? Look at the maps over several days to see where the pressure systems are heading. Is one coming your way? Low pressure usually means cloudy skies and precipitation. High pressure means fair weather. Remember that winds circulate clockwise around highs and counterclockwise around lows. What side of the high or low are you on? North winds are typically cool, while southerly winds are warm.

SHIFTING WINDS

A change in wind direction is a sign that a front is coming your way and that you can expect some rainy or snowy weather. Slow gentle precipitation usually falls before a warm front arrives. Short heavy bursts of rain or snow tell you a cold front is on the way.

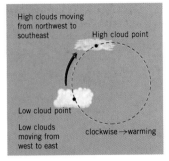

High clouds moving from northwest to southeast

High cloud point

Low cloud point

Low clouds moving from west to east

clockwise →warming

WATCHING THE CLOUDS

You can forecast the weather just by watching the clouds move! Look up at the sky. Where are the lower clouds blowing from? Where are the higher clouds blowing from? Draw an imaginary line from the low cloud point to the high cloud point. If your line goes in a clockwise direction (like the hands of a clock), warmer air is on the way. If your line is traveling in a counterclockwise direction, cooler air is coming.

FALLING BAROMETERS

Television meteorologists sometimes say "the barometer is falling" when they are predicting bad weather. They mean that a low-pressure system is on the way, bringing clouds and possibly rain or snow. They don't mean that barometers will be falling from the sky!

Tips for successful sky watching

- Look at the sky several times a day.
- Use a field guide like this one to identify the clouds.
- Record changes in wind direction and cloud type in your weather notebook.
- Be sure to record special events, like rainbows, blizzards, thunder and lightning, and hail.
- Compare your weather notes over a few days.
- Make a forecast and compare it with a professional meteorologist's prediction.

Making a weather station

Professional quality instruments may be more accurate, but there are simpler ones you can buy for home use, and it is possible even to make some of them yourself. This is a fun way to learn about weather.

Your at-home weather station should have the following instruments: a thermometer to measure temperature, a barometer to measure air pressure, an anemometer to measure wind speed, and a rain gauge to measure rainfall.

Anemometer

You can make an anemometer to record changes in wind speed (but a homemade anemometer is not accurate enough to tell you the actual wind speed). Here is how to make a simple one: Poke a drinking straw through a paper plate. Next, pound a nail partway into a wooden board and stand the straw on the nail. Then, staple three or four paper cups, one painted a bright color, onto the plate, equal distances apart. When the wind blows into the open ends of the cups, count how many spins the colored cup makes in one minute.

An anemometer made of wood and plastic cups

Barometer

Barometers keep track of air pressure. You can buy a barometer or you can make a simple one by stretching a piece of balloon over a glass jar and gluing a straw to the center of the balloon. Glue or tie a toothpick to the end of the straw. Set up an index card marked with "High" and "Low" lines near the toothpick's point.

When air pressure is high (which means fair weather), the toothpick will point up because air will be pressing down on the balloon. When air pressure is low (which means bad weather is coming), the toothpick will point down because air inside the jar will be pushing up against the balloon.

Rain gauge

To measure rain, all you need to do is put a jar outside before it starts raining. After the rain stops, measure how many inches of rain are in the jar. You can also use a jar to see how much water is in snow. Put an inch of snow in a jar, then bring it inside and let it melt. Heavy wet snow will have a lot more water in it than dry fluffy snow.

Using the field guide

Corona page 147

This section features 50 types of clouds, storms, and other weather events that occur in North America. Color photographs and details about each subject are included to help you identify what you see. The section begins with types of clouds (from high clouds to middle clouds to low clouds). Storms and events related to storms, like floods, come next. The last section of the field guide covers other things you might see in the sky that are related to weather, like haze, rainbows, and sky colors.

Crepuscular rays page 65

ICONS

These icons, which appear on each left-hand page, help you quickly find the subject you are looking for.

 Clouds

 Tropical Storms

 Drought

 Rainstorms

 Snow & Ice

 Pollution

 Tornadoes

 Floods

 Colors in the Sky

• **SUBJECT ICON**

This icon identifies the subject covered on the page.

• **NAME**

The name tells you what is discussed on the page.

• **BOX HEADING**

The box heading alerts you to other subjects or information covered in the box. This may be more information about the main subject or it may be about related subjects or things that are similar in some way to the main subject on the page.

MORE ABOUT CIRRUS

CIRRUS CLOUDS

Cirrus clouds form 3 miles (5 km) high or higher in the sky, where temperatures are always very cold. They are usually made of ice crystals and are often the first sign of an approaching storm. However, they can also form when strong winds knock off the tops of thunderstorm (cumulonimbus) clouds, indicating that a storm is breaking up.

LOOK FOR: Wispy, milky clouds in many shapes and sizes. Sometimes they appear as layers that give the sky a milky white color. Long stringy cirrus clouds like the ones in this photograph are called "mares' tails."

SEASON AND RANGE: Year-round, throughout North America.

CIRRUS FIBRATUS
These delicate feathery clouds often cover large areas of the sky, reducing the amount of sunlight that reaches the ground.

CIRRUS RADIATUS
These clouds have streamers—long ribbonlike bands that stretch across the sky and seem to point toward a spot on the distant horizon.

51

IDENTIFICATION CAPSULE •

The identification capsule covers all the details you need to identify a cloud, storm, or other type of weather.

• **SEASON AND RANGE**

The season and range listings tell you at a glance whether or not a type of weather is likely to occur in your area and also what times of year it can be seen.

CIRRUS CLOUDS

Cirrus clouds form 3 miles (5 km) high or higher in the sky, where temperatures are always very cold. They are usually made of ice crystals and are often the first sign of an approaching storm. However, they can also form when strong winds knock off the tops of thunderstorm (cumulonimbus) clouds, indicating that a storm is breaking up.

LOOK FOR: Wispy, milky clouds in many shapes and sizes. Sometimes they appear as layers that give the sky a milky white color. Long stringy cirrus clouds like the ones in this photograph are called "mares' tails."

SEASON AND RANGE: Year-round; throughout North America.

CIRRUS FIBRATUS
These delicate feathery clouds often cover large areas of the sky, reducing the amount of sunlight that reaches the ground.

CIRRUS RADIATUS
These clouds have streamers—long ribbonlike bands that stretch across the sky and seem to point toward a spot on the distant horizon.

51

These clouds are a sign of turbulence—strong irregular winds—in the upper atmosphere. They look grainy or patchy, and because they form in such strong winds, they do not usually stay in one place for long. Cirrocumulus clouds are a lot like cumulus clouds but they look smaller because they form at much higher altitudes.

LOOK FOR: Puffy white ripples that sometimes form rows across the sky. These are one of the most beautiful types of clouds. Look up often so you do not miss them!

SEASON AND RANGE: Year-round; throughout North America.

CIRROCUMULUS WITH IRIDESCENCE

Sometimes cirrocumulus clouds are made of supercooled water droplets (below 32°F, 0°C). When the droplets are all the same size, a colorful phenomenon called iridescence can occur. Iridescence is caused by sunlight or moonlight reflecting off the droplets and breaking up into multicolored fragments of light.

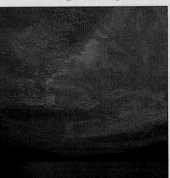

CIRROCUMULUS AT SUNRISE/SUNSET

When the sun is near the horizon, either rising or setting, it lights up the undersides of cirrocumulus clouds, causing a beautiful display of color.

53

Cirrostratus clouds

Cirrostratus are high-altitude layered clouds that cover large portions of the sky. They often have no definite shape and are seen only as a change in the sky's color from blue to milky white. They do not block out the sun like other stratus-type clouds do. Cirrostratus clouds are made of tiny ice crystals. They usually produce a halo, a rainbow-colored ring around the sun or moon, and are a good indication of rain or snow to come.

LOOK FOR: Large, high, white to light gray layers without distinct shapes or edges.

SEASON AND RANGE: Year-round; throughout North America. Particularly common in winter in northern areas.

CIRROSTRATUS FIBRATUS
These clouds appear as streaks or filaments strung out across the sky. Note their fuzzy edges, which are typical of ice crystal clouds.

SUNDOGS AND HALOS
Colorful halos and sundogs (bright colorful spots on either side of the sun) often appear with cirrostratus clouds. You can safely observe these spectacular sky colors if you block out the sun by holding your hand out at arm's length from your body. Be sure not to look directly into the sun!

CONTRAILS

MOISTURE IN THE AIR

In dry air, contrails evaporate and quickly disappear. If a contrail keeps its shape for a long time, that means there is a lot of moisture high in the atmosphere.

Contrail is short for condensation trail. These man-made clouds form high in the atmosphere when water vapor (a gas) from the exhaust of jet airplanes condenses into ice crystals. At first they look like thin bright lines but they later spread out and cut a wide path across the sky.

LOOK FOR: Straight narrow white lines or wide fuzzy grayish bands high in the atmosphere.

SEASON AND RANGE: Year-round; throughout North America wherever planes fly. Especially common in areas of heavy air traffic.

DIFFUSION

Gusty high-altitude winds can nibble away at the edges of contrails and eventually break them up—a phenomenon called diffusion.

57

Altocumulus are middle-altitude clouds that indicate warm air rising. They also indicate increasing amounts of water vapor and often occur in advance of an approaching storm. They are made up mostly of water droplets and form anywhere between 1 and 3 miles (1½–5 km) high. If altocumulus clouds are present during sunrise or sunset, get ready for a colorful sky show!

LOOK FOR: Individual white or gray clouds of differing shapes. They tend to clump together and form various patterns.

SEASON AND RANGE: Year-round; throughout North America.

CLOUD STREETS
Altocumulus clouds sometimes line up in the direction of the wind and extend side-by-side for hundreds of miles. These "cloud streets" are most often observed over the ocean.

MACKEREL SKY
Dense patches of altocumulus clouds can form patterns that look like scales on a fish; this is called a mackerel sky. The saying "mackerel sky, mackerel sky, not long wet and not long dry" tells us that a mackerel sky means rainy weather, and the rain will keep stopping and starting.

59

Altostratus clouds signal the approach of a warm front, which means that rain or snow is probably on the way. These are middle-level clouds, formed mostly of water droplets with some supercooled droplets as well. If you see altostratus clouds, keep an eye on the sky for changing wind directions and weather conditions!

Look for: Dreary gray sheet-like clouds that cover the entire sky. Altostratus look smooth and have no distinguishing shapes or features.

Season and range: Year-round; throughout North America.

ALTOSTRATUS AT SUNSET
Altostratus clouds do not produce halos or sundogs like cirrostratus clouds do. This is because altostratus are formed from water droplets, while cirrostratus are formed from ice crystals.

WATERY SUN
The sun can be seen shining through altostratus clouds but only as a faint yellow disk. This dimly visible sun, which looks wet around the edges, is often referred to as a "watery sun."

61

STRATUS CLOUDS

Stratus clouds make for a dreary day. They form in large flat layers low in the sky and usually completely block out the sun. Depending on the temperature, stratus clouds can be made of water droplets or ice crystals.

LOOK FOR: Light to dark gray cloud layers at very low altitudes. Stratus clouds look a lot like fog except they do not reach ground level.

SEASON AND RANGE: Year-round; throughout North America. Most common over the ocean, along coastal areas, and during winter in eastern areas.

NIMBOSTRATUS

A dark stratus cloud that produces rain or snow is called nimbostratus. Sometimes the rain can be such a fine light drizzle you can barely feel it. When the precipitation stops, the cloud becomes stratus again.

VIEWED FROM ABOVE

Stratus clouds are flat on the bottom, indicating low levels of turbulence. The tops can be quite bumpy, however. Look out the window the next time you are in an airplane!

63

 # Stratocumulus clouds

These are low-altitude clouds that form when lots of moisture exists in air that has only small amounts of turbulence. Sometimes stratocumulus clouds are seen just before the sky clears after a storm.

LOOK FOR: Large patches of white to gray clouds mottled with darker gray. They look a lot like cumulus clouds but are darker and more clumped together and leave very little sky showing. Stratocumulus clouds sometimes form rippling rows.

SEASON AND RANGE: Year-round, throughout North America. Very common over the ocean, along coasts, and during winter in eastern areas.

CREPUSCULAR RAYS

Sunbeams shining through gaps in stratocumulus clouds are called crepuscular rays. They are caused by sunlight scattering around dust and other particles in the air.

STRATOCUMULUS AT SUNSET

These low-altitude clouds can be highly variable in their shape, size, and coloring—they are often quite striking during sunrises and sunsets.

65

FOG

Fog is a cloud that forms at ground level. This can be a dangerous weather event, reducing visibility to such an extent that it becomes unsafe to drive a car or fly a plane. But fog also gives people the opportunity to walk around with their heads in the clouds! Fog is usually made of tiny water droplets but in very cold places, like Alaska, ice fog can form from ice crystals. This photograph shows advection fog, which forms when the wind moves very moist air over a cooler surface.

RADIATION FOG

Radiation fog forms when nighttime or early morning cooling condenses water vapor into liquid droplets. This type of fog usually evaporates, or "burns off," by mid-morning.

VALLEY FOG

In hilly or mountainous areas, cold evening air slides downhill. The cooling air causes fog to fill the valleys—a beautiful morning sight in the mountains.

LOOK FOR: Thick gray clouds at ground level. Of course, if you find yourself in the middle of a fog cloud, you probably will not be able to actually see it!

SEASON AND RANGE: Year-round, throughout North America. Advection fog is especially common in coastal areas.

67

Cumulus clouds

INDUSTRIAL CUMULUS
The water vapor in smokestack plumes can condense to form industrial "cumulus plumulus" clouds.

These are the pretty, fair-weather clouds that appear on a beautiful day—the ones you might look at to find hidden pictures. At low altitudes, cumulus clouds form from water droplets, but the upper portions of tall cumulus clouds are made of ice crystals.

Look for: Individual puffy white clouds in a clear blue sky. Cumulus clouds look like cotton balls with flat bottoms and rounded sides and tops.

Season and range: Year-round; throughout North America. Especially common during summer.

TOWERING CUMULUS
Lots of moisture and rising air cause cumulus clouds to grow and grow into towering cumulus congestus clouds. If they continue growing, these powerful clouds will soon give rise to a thunderstorm.

The tallest clouds of all, cumulonimbus grow from near ground level to altitudes as high as 70,000 feet (21,000 m). They form when a towering cumulus congestus cloud continues growing until it flattens out at the top into an anvil shape. Cumulonimbus clouds are made up of ice crystals in their upper portions and water droplets in their lower portions.

LOOK FOR: Tall billowing white clouds that often have very dark bases. The bases are sharply defined, while the flattened anvil-shaped tops have the fuzzy appearance of ice crystal clouds.

SEASON AND RANGE: Spring, summer, and fall; throughout North America, except in very cold areas.

CUMULONIMBUS WITH PILEUS
Cumulonimbus clouds are huge masses of liquid and solid water and are an obstacle to wind. Strong winds that flow over the tops of these clouds can freeze into a saucer-shaped pileus cloud.

ANVIL-SHAPED TOPS
The anvil shape of the top of a cumulonimbus cloud is caused by the cloud pushing up against the stratosphere, the second layer of the earth's atmosphere. The stable stratospheric air resists this invasion from below, pushing back down and flattening the cloud top in the process.

Cumulonimbus clouds that produce damaging winds, large hail, or tornadoes are called severe thunderstorm clouds. The sky beneath a severe thunderstorm gets very dark, because the tall cloud blocks out most of the sun's light.

Look for: Dark ominous clouds, high winds, heavy rain, lightning, and sometimes large hail or even tornadoes. Always observe these clouds from a safe distance. If one is nearby, stay indoors and away from windows and metal objects.

Season and range: Spring, summer, and occasionally fall; throughout North America. Most common in central U.S.

LATENT HEAT

Large amounts of heat are released into the air when water vapor condenses and forms a thunderstorm cloud. This heat is called latent heat. Latent heat helps the cloud grow taller by warming the air and causing it to rise even more. It provides energy for severe turbulent winds, hail, and tornadoes.

MESOCYCLONES

A mesocyclone is an area of spinning winds that can occur inside a severe thunderstorm. These strong gusty winds often produce tornadoes. Some very severe thunderstorms can have two or three mesocyclones at the same time. (For more about mesocyclones, see page 100.)

73

MAMMATUS CLOUDS

The air that rises to make cumulonimbus clouds so tall also pushes downward to form mammatus clouds. These clouds look a lot like a cow's udders hanging down from the sky. Mammatus clouds can indicate severe weather because they form from well-developed thunderstorms.

LOOK FOR: Bulging clouds hanging down from part of a cumulonimbus cloud.

SEASON AND RANGE: Spring, summer, and fall; throughout North America, except in very cold areas.

MAMMATUS AT SUNSET
Mammatus are one of the most spectacular cloud types. The descending pockets of warm air can look especially eerie just after sunset.

MAMMATUS UNDER A CUMULONIMBUS ANVIL
The downward-moving air that is necessary to form mammatus clouds can occur under the anvil shape in the cloud's upper portion as well as at the cloud base. Look for mammatus clouds high up in a thunderstorm's anvil region.

75

GUST FRONT CLOUDS

Thunderstorm (cumulonimbus) clouds are very tall because large amounts of warm humid air rise several miles above the ground. But what goes up must come down. Gust front clouds are caused by cool air moving downward out of a strong thunderstorm. Also called cumulus arcus, they are a sign of strong winds and changing wind direction.

LOOK FOR: A long billowing line of dark clouds, often very low to the ground. Gust front clouds look ominous and threatening.

SEASON AND RANGE: Spring, summer, and fall. Common in eastern regions and occasionally in other mountainous areas.

GUST FRONT WINDS
Strong wind shifts occur near gust fronts and present a serious hazard to aircraft, especially during takeoffs and landings.

LOW GUST FRONTS
Gust front clouds in humid areas can occur only a few hundred feet above the ground. In drier areas, they form at altitudes of over 10,000 feet (3,000 m).

77

LENTICULAR CLOUDS

Lenticular clouds indicate wavelike air motions in the atmosphere. The saucer-shaped clouds form at the tops, or crests, of the waves.

The wind cannot blow through mountains; it must flow over or around them. Unusual cloud formations can result when mountains interfere with air flow. These are called orographic clouds. This photograph shows the most common type of orographic cloud—the altocumulus lenticularis, or lenticular, cloud.

LOOK FOR: Clouds shaped like saucers. These smooth rounded clouds can appear to pile on top of each other. They have sometimes been mistaken for UFOs!

SEASON AND RANGE: Year-round; in any mountainous area. Especially common in Colorado during winter.

CREST CLOUDS

As air rises over the top of a tall mountain ridge, a cloud can form at the top. These crest clouds can sometimes hover over a ridge for several hours.

79

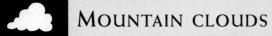

MOUNTAIN CLOUDS

Orographic clouds and precipitation occur most often on the upwind side of a mountain range, which is the side from which the wind is blowing. The downwind, or lee, side remains quite dry. This side is called the rain shadow.

LOOK FOR: Precipitating clouds upwind of a mountain range. The precipitation usually stops near the mountain's peak.

SEASON AND RANGE: Year-round; in any mountainous area.

VALLEY FOG

Slow-moving air can get trapped in mountain valleys. When the air cools, fog forms. This fog remains until the wind becomes stronger or until sunlight evaporates it. (For more about fog, see page 66.)

WAVE CLOUDS

Air flows over mountains in wavelike patterns. When it passes through large multiple mountain ranges, the air waves and the clouds they carry can become twisted into strange pretzel-like shapes.

81

Although air is invisible, you can see its complex movements by watching the clouds. Breaking waves, just like those found on ocean beaches, can also be found in the atmosphere. These are called Kelvin-Helmholtz wave clouds. They indicate strong turbulence at high altitudes. Wouldn't it be fun to surf them?

LOOK FOR: A line of circular white clouds that look like waves cresting on a beach.

SEASON AND RANGE: Year-round; throughout North America.

NOCTILUCENT CLOUDS

These wavy, bluish-white clouds are occasionally visible high in the mesosphere, about 50 miles (80 km) above the earth's surface. They are so thin that stars shine brightly through them. Noctilucent clouds can occur year-round and are most easily seen at twilight, near the north and south polar regions.

PYROCUMULUS CLOUDS

During forest fires or wildfires, burning vegetation releases large amounts of water vapor into the air. This water vapor rises with the hot air to form puffy pyrocumulus clouds (*pyro* is the Latin word for "fire"). These clouds form mainly in summer and fall, wherever forest fires and wildfires occur.

MIXED CLOUDS

Sometimes as many as three or four types of clouds can be seen in the sky at the same time. When this happens, identifying each cloud can be tricky. In this photograph, both cirrus and cumulus clouds are visible. Both of these cloud types indicate that air is rising and sinking, which may lead to thunderstorm development.

Look for: Thin patches of wispy cirrus clouds at high altitudes and thicker puffy cumulus clouds below. Mixed clouds are easiest to observe when the lower-altitude clouds are cumulus, which leave wide spaces of clear air.

Season and range: Year-round; throughout North America.

Cumulonimbus, Cumulus, and Cirrus

On warm humid days, full-blown cumulonimbus clouds can often be seen together with cirrus, as well as small cumulus clouds that may soon develop into cumulonimbus clouds (or thunderstorms).

Cumulus and Cumulus Congestus

Moisture and rising air cause cumulus clouds to develop into towering cumulus congestus clouds, which can in turn become cumulonimbus clouds.

85

In this aerial photograph, stratus and cumulus clouds share the sky. When stratus clouds form at lower altitudes, it can be difficult—sometimes impossible—to see what is happening above them. An airplane is a great place to see the clouds. Although it may look cloudy and gray from the ground, airplanes fly above the clouds, where skies are blue and visibility is good.

LOOK FOR: High-altitude cumulus clouds indicate fair weather in the upper atmosphere. Nearer to ground level, however, layered patches of stratus clouds threaten rain.

SEASON AND RANGE: Year-round; throughout North America.

LENTICULAR AND CIRRUS CLOUDS

In mountainous areas, lenticular and cirrus clouds can occasionally be seen together. These clouds make beautiful and interesting combinations of shapes and colors.

CIRRUS AND CUMULUS CLOUDS

Cirrus and cumulus are two of the most common cloud types and are often seen together in the sky.

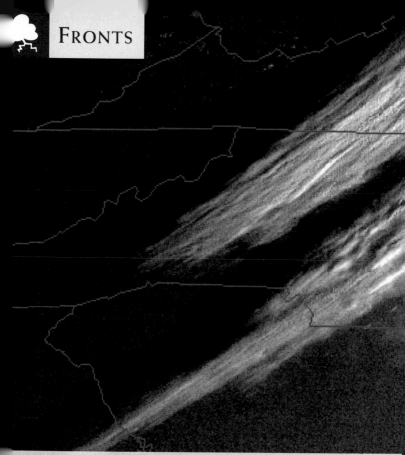

FRONTS

Fronts are the atmosphere's battleground between warm and cold air. The weather is often quite different on either side of a front. One side might be cool and dry with northwest winds, while the other side is warm and humid with winds from the south. When a warm front arrives, it often brings steady rain or snow; a cold front may bring a short but heavy rainstorm or snowstorm. This photograph shows a weak front passing over the eastern United States. The clouds, stretching over several states, are high clouds probably made of ice crystals.

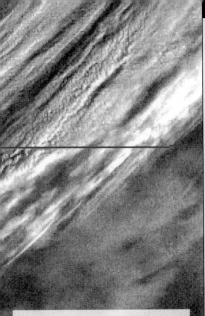

PRECIPITATION

Warm air rises as it meets cold air, forming clouds and precipitation. This satellite photograph shows thunderstorms building over Georgia. The bumpy-looking cloud tops show that updrafts inside the clouds are causing the clouds to grow upward. Soon the updrafts will slow down and the cloud tops will spread out in the anvil shape.

LOOK FOR: Fronts are easy to see in satellite photographs, appearing as long bands of clouds. From the ground, a sequence of high clouds (cirrus or cirrostratus) changing over several hours to middle clouds (altostratus or altocumulus) and later changing to low clouds signals an approaching warm front. Look for dropping temperatures, dropping air pressures, and shifting winds when a cold front is moving in.

SEASON AND RANGE: Year-round; throughout North America.

CIRRUS CLOUDS AND WARM FRONTS

Cirrus clouds sometimes mean a warm front (and rain or snow) is on the way. Watch for middle-level clouds and then low clouds to follow.

89

RAINSTORMS

Rain falls in many different ways: a misty drizzle, a brief shower, a steady daylong stream, or a drenching downpour. Drizzle, the smallest of all raindrops, is 1/50 inch (1/20 cm) across. Typical raindrops are about 1/12 inch (1/5 cm) across. The largest drops ever measured were nearly 1/4 inch (3/5 cm) across, but drops this large usually break apart as they fall.

LOOK FOR: Nimbostratus clouds bring light showers or steady rain. Cumulonimbus clouds bring heavy rain, thunder, and lightning. Darkening daytime skies tell you that a tall cumulonimbus cloud is nearby, blocking out the sun. Decreasing air pressures and rising humidity are good indicators of approaching rain.

SEASON AND RANGE: Year-round, especially spring and summer. Throughout North America, but not often in desert areas.

DOWNPOURS
Heavy rain is called a downpour. Downpours can last from a few minutes to several weeks. Flooding often occurs when rain-soaked rivers overflow their banks.

SHOWERS
Rain that starts and stops abruptly is called a shower. Showers sometimes affect very small areas—it may rain on only one side of the street!

91

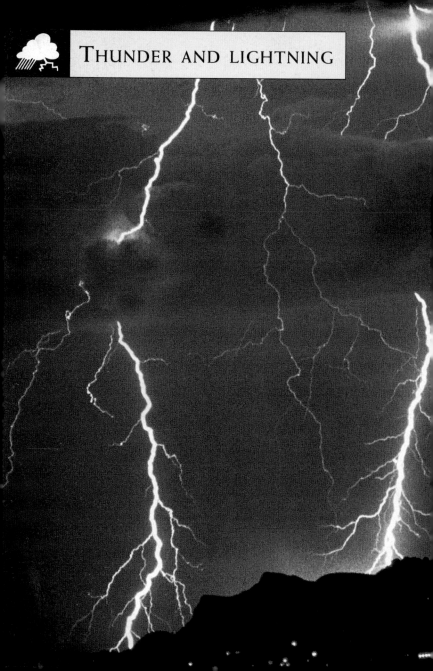

THUNDER AND LIGHTNING

Lightning is a huge, hot spark of electricity that shoots out of a thunderstorm cloud. Thunder is the sound made when air heated by lightning explodes.

LOOK FOR: Puffy white cumulus clouds that grow taller and form cumulus congestus (towering cumulus) clouds, which grow still taller and flatten out at the top, forming anvil-shaped thunderheads.

SEASON AND RANGE: Mostly during spring and summer, but year-round in warmer climates. Throughout North America, but more frequently in warmer climates.

CAUTION: Lightning is deadly. It is best to go indoors when lightning is nearby. If caught outdoors, stay away from high places and do not go under a tree. Crouch down on two feet; do not lie flat.

CLOUD-TO-GROUND LIGHTNING

Cloud-to-ground lightning is the most dangerous kind of lightning. (In the United States, around 100 people are killed by this type of lightning each year.) The bolt of lightning goes from the cloud to the ground (or often the tallest object in the area).

HOW FAR AWAY?

Light travels 186,000 miles (300,000 km) per second, while sound travels only ⅕ mile (³⁄₁₀ km) per second. That is why you often see a flash of lightning but do not hear the thunder until several seconds later. If a lightning flash occurs a mile away from you, it will be five seconds before you hear the thunder. Count the number of seconds between when you first see a lightning flash and when you hear the thunder. Divide this number by five and you will know how many miles away the lightning bolt hit.

93

LIGHTNING

Not all lightning hits the earth. Lightning that travels inside a single cloud is called in-cloud lightning. Cloud-to-cloud lightning goes from one cloud to another. This type of lightning is a hazard to aircraft.

LOOK FOR: Flashes of lightning along the bottom of a cumulonimbus cloud or from one cloud to another. Sometimes a cloud seems to glow from within.

SEASON AND RANGE: Mostly during spring and summer, but year-round in warmer climates. Throughout North America, but more frequently in warmer climates.

BALL LIGHTNING

Ball lightning is a mysterious form of lightning that appears to float or dart about in the air. These bright red or yellow balls last for a second or two before exploding with a loud bang.

LIGHTNING DAMAGE

Lightning strikes with extremely powerful force. It can split trees, damage houses, and start fires.

95

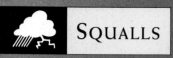

SQUALLS

Squalls are rapidly moving lines of showers or thunderstorms that form along a cold front. Many squall lines are more than 600 miles (970 km) long. Like ordinary thunderstorms, squalls may produce strong winds, large hail, and tornadoes.

LOOK FOR: A line of dark clouds. Winds may become strong as the squall line approaches, followed by sudden rain or snow.

SEASON AND RANGE: Mostly during spring and summer; throughout North America. Strong squall lines often occur in the Great Plains.

SQUALLS AND COLD FRONTS

Squalls can form in the warm humid air ahead of a cold front. It may take a few hours for the cold air to arrive after a squall line passes overhead.

SNOW SQUALLS

Winter squalls can produce heavy snows. Snow squalls often occur along the downwind shores of large lakes such as the Great Lakes. Marquette, in Michigan's Upper Peninsula, often has heavy snowfall from squalls coming in from Lake Superior.

97

MICROBURSTS

Microbursts are powerful wind gusts caused by strong blasts of downward-moving air below cumulonimbus clouds. The fast-moving air hits the ground and spreads out in all directions. The air inside a microburst comes from the top of the troposphere (the first layer of the earth's atmosphere), several miles above the ground. Microbursts usually last a few minutes or less.

WET OR DRY

Microbursts can be either wet or dry. Wet microbursts are accompanied by heavy rainfall. Dry microbursts occur in dry areas underneath cumulonimbus clouds.

MICROBURSTS AND AIRPLANES

Several serious airplane crashes have been caused by microbursts, which are especially dangerous to a plane during takeoff and landing. Many airports have special equipment to warn of nearby microbursts.

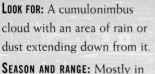

LOOK FOR: A cumulonimbus cloud with an area of rain or dust extending down from it.

SEASON AND RANGE: Mostly in spring and summer; wherever thunderstorms are found.

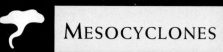

A powerful area of spinning upward-moving air inside a cumulonimbus cloud or thunderstorm is called a mesocyclone. Mesocyclones generally start in the middle of the cloud and stretch down toward the ground. As a mesocyclone spins faster it may produce a tornado.

LOOK FOR: Slowly spinning clouds during a nasty looking thunderstorm.

SEASON AND RANGE: Mostly spring and early summer; everywhere thunderstorms are found, but most often in the Great Plains.

WALL CLOUDS

A wall cloud forms when a rotating mesocyclone drops beneath the base of a cumulonimbus cloud. The wall cloud is the portion of the cumulonimbus cloud's base that drops down toward the ground. This is a sign that a tornado is developing.

UPDRAFTS AND DOWNDRAFTS

Mesocyclones occur in the updraft region of a thunderstorm—the area of upward-moving air. The precipitation occurs in another part of the storm, the downdraft region, where air is pulled down toward the ground.

TORNADOES

A funnel cloud (a cone-shaped cloud) is a swiftly rotating column of air, called a vortex, that drops out of a severe thunderstorm, or cumulonimbus, cloud. A funnel cloud that reaches the ground is called a tornado. Since air is invisible, the vortex that we can see consists of water droplets, dust, and debris sucked up from the ground.

LOOK FOR: A spiraling column of air dropping from the base of a cumulonimbus cloud. It is wider near the cloud and narrower toward the ground. Flying debris and noise like a freight train are other signs that a tornado is nearby. Take shelter immediately.

SEASON AND RANGE: Spring and summer; everywhere thunderstorms are found, but mostly in central U.S.

CAUTION: When tornado warnings are issued for your area, take shelter in the basement or in the center of a building. Stay away from windows.

FUNNEL CLOUDS

Most tornadoes start and end as a funnel cloud, but not all funnel clouds become tornadoes. Even so, you should always seek shelter if you spot a funnel cloud. The spinning winds inside a tornado can reach 300 miles (480 km) per hour!

DEADLY FORCE

Tornadoes can lift animals and cars into the air. The deadliest tornado on record in the United States was the tri-state tornado outbreak of March 18, 1925. Several tornadoes demolished portions of Missouri, Illinois, and Indiana, killing 747 people and injuring over 2,000 more.

WATERSPOUTS

DROPPING FROM CLOUDS

Like tornadoes, some waterspouts come from severe thunderstorm clouds. Most, however, drop out of small thunderstorms or even cumulus congestus (towering cumulus) clouds.

A rotating column of air that develops over water is called a waterspout. Smaller than its cousin the tornado, a waterspout has weaker winds, usually of speeds less than 50 miles (80 km) per hour. The shallow warm waters of the Florida Keys are a great place to look for waterspouts. They can also be found on the Great Lakes.

LOOK FOR: A spinning column of water stretching down from a cumulonimbus cloud to a large body of water such as a lake, wide river, or ocean.

SEASON AND RANGE: Spring and summer in northern areas; year-round in southern U.S. Mainly in coastal areas, but also near large lakes and rivers.

TORNADOES ON WATER

In coastal areas, tornadoes sometimes form over land and move out over the water, becoming waterspouts.

105

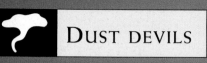

Small whirlwinds of dust form in dry areas such as deserts. Although they look like tornadoes, dust devils are not formed by thunderstorms and do not drop from the sky to the ground. Dust devils are caused by swirling winds that rise with the warm air found over the ground.

LOOK FOR: A spinning column of dust stretching up from the ground.

SEASON AND RANGE: Summer and autumn; usually in dry desert areas.

DUST DEVILS AND CLOUDS

Cumulus clouds sometimes form over dust devils. This can trick people into thinking they see a tornado. The same updraft (rising air) that creates a dust devil can also cause a cumulus cloud to form.

HOW POWERFUL?

Dust devils are nowhere near as powerful as tornadoes. Most are small and last only a few minutes, but stronger ones have actually knocked over mobile homes and damaged the roofs of small buildings.

107

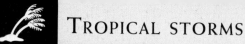

Tropical storms form over warm ocean waters. They begin as a tropical disturbance, which is nothing more than a cluster of big thunderstorms. When this growing storm begins to rotate, it becomes a tropical depression. When wind speeds reach 40 miles (65 km) per hour it is called a tropical storm. Tropical storms cover a huge area (sometimes 1,000 miles, or 1,600 km, across) and take a day or more to pass over a particular place. This photograph shows Tropical Storm Cosme (July 1995) over the Pacific Ocean.

LOOK FOR: A large storm over warm ocean waters with heavy rainfall and high wind speeds. Decreasing air pressure and high waves also signal an approaching tropical storm.

SEASON AND RANGE: Mainly late summer through fall. Tropical storms form over warm ocean waters, such as the Gulf of Mexico, the Caribbean Sea, and the tropical Atlantic and Pacific Oceans.

TROPICAL STORM OR HURRICANE?

When wind speeds reach 74 miles (119 km) per hour, a tropical storm becomes a hurricane. Like hurricanes, each tropical storm is given its own name. Hurricanes and tropical storms get their energy from the water that evaporates from the ocean surface. When the moist tropical air rises and condenses into cloud droplets, huge amounts of heat are released into the storm.

TROPICAL STORM DAMAGE

Not all tropical storms develop into full-fledged hurricanes. Tropical storms can cause a lot of damage though, especially with strong winds, high waves, and flooding.

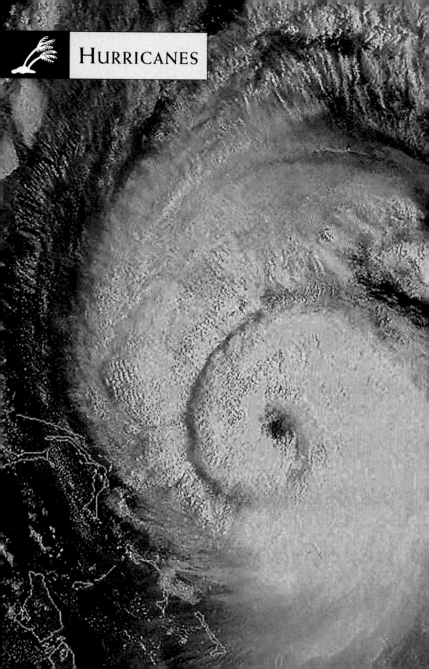

At the center of a hurricane is the eye, a hole 10 to 100 miles (15–160 km) wide in the center of the storm. The skies are nearly clear and the winds are light when the eye is passing overhead. Surrounding the eye is the eye wall, a bank of clouds containing the highest winds. Spiraling bands of cumulonimbus clouds around the eye wall bring heavy rains. This photograph shows Hurricane Fran (September 1996) off the coast of Florida.

LOOK FOR: A large tropical storm with very strong winds and heavy rain.

SEASON AND RANGE: Mainly late summer and autumn; season peaks in September. Hurricanes form over warm tropical ocean waters but may travel thousands of miles.

CAUTION: Keep a battery-powered radio nearby and listen carefully to watches and warnings issued by the National Hurricane Center. Be prepared to evacuate.

HURRICANE DAMAGE

After reaching land, a hurricane's source of energy is cut off, and the storm begins to die out. Even so, the heavy rains and high winds can cause incredible damage. To make matters worse, hurricanes often spawn tornadoes after reaching land.

STORM SURGES

Hurricanes cause the sea level to rise, sometimes by 10 feet (3 m) or more. This is called a storm surge. Storm surges combine with heavy rainfall, daily tides, and pounding waves to create massive flooding during hurricanes. (For more about storm surges, see page 128.)

111

ICE STORMS

When temperatures below a raining cloud are very cold, the raindrops become supercooled, which means they cool to below 32°F (0°C) and freeze when they hit the ground and other objects. Called freezing rain, precipitation from these ice storms covers streets, houses, and trees with layers of heavy ice.

LOOK FOR: Falling rain when the temperature is below freezing (32°F, 0°C).

SEASON AND RANGE: Winter and early spring; throughout North America, but rare in southern areas.

ICE STORM DAMAGE
Trees and electrical power lines are often damaged as they become weighted down with heavy ice.

SLEET
Sleet forms when falling snow melts and then refreezes before it hits the ground. It consists of small pellets of ice that bounce and make tapping sounds when they hit the ground.

HAIL

Like sleet and freezing rain, hail is a mixture of liquid and frozen precipitation. Formed inside cumulonimbus clouds, hailstones are composed of layers of ice and can become quite large when strong gusts of upward-moving air keep them inside the cloud. As they blow around in the cloud they collide with raindrops, adding layers and growing before they fall to the earth.

LOOK FOR: Severe thunderstorms with heavy rains and strong winds.

SEASON AND RANGE: Late spring, summer, and early fall; everywhere thunderstorms are found.

HOW BIG?

Hailstones can be the size of marbles, golfballs, or even baseballs. Hail can cause a lot of damage. Imagine standing in a field being pelted by thousands of golfballs flung from the sky!

HAILSTONE RINGS

Slicing open a hailstone reveals its structure of rings. Each ring is a layer that was added during one of its up-and-down trips through a cumulonimbus cloud. Count the rings and you will know how many trips the hailstone took!

115

FROST

Ice crystals that form on a surface, such as the ground or the leaves of plants, are called frost. Frost forms when the air temperature drops below freezing and the water vapor in the air freezes into ice crystals.

LOOK FOR: A thin layer of delicate, feathery ice crystals on the ground, leaves, rooftops, cars, windows, and other surfaces.

SEASON AND RANGE: Late autumn, winter, early spring; throughout North America, but rare in southern U.S.

FROST INDOORS

Frost forms on the inside of windows because the warm air inside a building contains water vapor that freezes on the cold glass. If you look at the sun through a frost-covered windowpane you may see a kaleidoscope of colors. The frozen crystals act as tiny prisms and produce the brilliant colors.

FROST ON CROPS

Frost is devastating to crops. When temperatures drop below freezing (32°F, 0°C), the water inside leaves and stems freezes. Some farmers burn large drums of oil in their orchards on cold nights to ward off frost.

117

SNOW

Snow forms when cloud temperatures are below freezing (32°F, 0°C). Depending on temperature and humidity, snowflakes can have lots of different shapes. Falling snowflakes can collide with raindrops, making sticky mixtures of ice and water. Winter storms are not as destructive as tornadoes or hurricanes, yet they can bring entire regions to a standstill.

LOOK FOR: Cold temperatures and nimbostratus clouds. Large heavy flakes indicate warmer temperatures and more moisture; dry brittle flakes indicate colder temperatures and less moisture.

SEASON AND RANGE: Mainly winter; throughout North America, but rare in southern U.S.

CAUTION: During cold weather it is important to cover up all exposed skin to avoid frostbite (frozen skin). Windy cold weather is particularly dangerous.

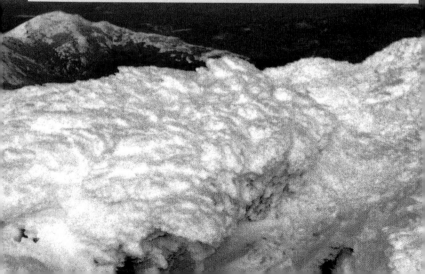

FLURRIES AND SQUALLS

Snow that starts and stops, sometimes
many times over, is called a flurry or
snow shower. More intense brief
snowfall, sometimes accumulating to
several inches or more, is called a snow
squall.

LAKE EFFECT

Large lakes often remain unfrozen during
winter. Since lake water temperatures can
be as much as 40°F (22°C) warmer than
the air temperature, lots of water
evaporates over a lake. When carried
ashore by wind this moist air cools,
condenses, and produces large amounts
of snow. Areas near the Great Lakes,
Great Salt Lake, and Canada's Hudson
Bay all receive considerable snow from
the lake effect.

119

BLIZZARDS

The combination of heavy snowfall, cold temperatures, and strong winds causes a blizzard. Since blowing snow greatly reduces visibility, and temperatures combined with the wind can make it cold enough for frostbite, it is dangerous to be outside during a blizzard.

LOOK FOR: Low visibility, strong winds, and snow moving sideways.

SEASON AND RANGE: Mostly winter; throughout North America, but rare in southern U.S.

NOR'EASTERS

Most of the snow in New England and the mid-Atlantic states comes from northeasters (often called nor'easters), storms with strong northeast winds that form over the Atlantic Ocean. These storms often dump large amounts of snow on the highly populated east coast.

BLIZZARD OF '88

The famous blizzard of March 11–14, 1888, blanketed the eastern United States and dumped up to 58 inches (147 cm) of snow on New York State. In New York City snow drifts reached higher than second-story windows.

121

AVALANCHES

AVALANCHE DAMAGE

More than 1,200 avalanches are reported in the United States each year. An avalanche in Washington in 1910 caused several railroad cars to plummet 150 feet (45 m), killing 100 passengers.

In an avalanche, up to 100,000 tons of snow can cascade down a mountainside at speeds of over 60 miles (100 km) per hour and destroy everything in its path.

LOOK FOR: A new fall of loose powdery snow on a hard icy base of older snow may cause an avalanche on steep slopes.

SEASON AND RANGE: Winter, spring, and summer; in mountainous areas.

CAUTION: When skiing or snowmobiling in mountainous areas, avoid steep slopes. Always stay out of areas that have avalanche warnings posted.

AVALANCHE CHUTES

Avalanche chutes are areas where trees have been knocked down by thousands of tons of tumbling snow. They are evidence of past avalanches.

123

Floods—too much water in places that are not normally under water—are responsible for nearly half of all deaths caused by natural disasters worldwide. Many floods occur in the spring, when melting snow, heavy rains, and waterlogged soil cause rivers to rise so much that they flow over their banks onto the surrounding land.

LOOK FOR: Heavy rains, melting snows, and rising river levels. Watch your rain gauge if rain continues for several days.

SEASON AND RANGE: Mainly spring but also summer; throughout North America, especially in low-lying areas near rivers.

CAUTION: To keep safe during a flood, stay out of gushing water if it is above your knees. If you are in a car that stalls in deep water, get out and move to high ground.

HURRICANE FLOODING

Hurricanes often cause flooding—even in areas the hurricane does not hit! As hurricanes weaken over land, they turn into low-pressure systems that can bring heavy rains far inland. These rains can cause rivers to overflow and even turn streets into rushing streams.

FLOOD OF 1993

The Mississippi River flood of 1993 was the longest and costliest flood in U.S. history. During the winter of 1992–93, heavy snows had blanketed much of the midwestern United States. Heavy spring rains helped melt the snow, which drained into swollen streams and rivers. Widespread flooding continued throughout the summer, covering 16,000 square miles (26,000 square km) in nine states, causing $6.5 billion in crop damage and destroying 45,000 homes.

Floodwaters that rise swiftly with no warning are called flash floods. They often occur after intense rainfall from slow-moving thunderstorms. In narrow canyons and valleys, floodwaters flow faster than on flatter ground and can be quite destructive.

LOOK FOR: Slow-moving thunderstorms with extremely heavy rains.

SEASON AND RANGE: Mainly spring and summer; throughout North America, especially areas with streams and rivers in narrow valleys or steep canyons.

CAUTION: If floodwaters rise above the banks of a river or stream, climb to higher ground immediately. It is a good idea to carry a battery-powered radio to listen for warnings.

CANYON FLOODS

Flash floods often occur in mountainous areas where narrow canyons and gorges funnel the water into a pounding torrent that destroys everything in its path. Flash floods also occur in deserts where hard dry soil cannot absorb much rain after a heavy thunderstorm.

FLOOD DAMAGE

Flash floods sweep through quickly—but can cause a lot of damage. During a four-hour period on July 31, 1976, severe thunderstorms dumped 12 inches (30 cm) of rain over the Big Thompson Canyon in Colorado's Rocky Mountains. Gentle mountain creeks turned into raging rivers that swallowed up tents, cars, and houses. The flooding caused $35 million in damage and claimed 135 lives.

127

A storm surge is a rise in the ocean level caused by the high winds and low pressure of an offshore tropical storm or hurricane. Storm surges hit the coast as a wall of water up to 25 feet (8 m) high that can destroy everything in its path.

HOW THE SURGE FORMS

A storm surge begins as a hill of water that forms under a hurricane as extremely low pressures cause surrounding air to rush toward the storm. The mound of water spirals downward and gets carried toward shore. Millions of gallons of ocean water spill onto land when a hurricane reaches the coast, causing extensive flooding and destruction.

SURGE DANGER

Surging ocean waters generally do not come closer to land than a mile or two from the coast, but flooding from heavy hurricane rains can extend over 100 miles (160 km) inland. The storm surge is the deadliest part of a hurricane.

LOOK FOR: An approaching tropical storm or hurricane, or a fast rise in tidewaters to high levels.

SEASON AND RANGE: Late summer and early fall; in coastal areas, especially in the tropics.

129

DROUGHT

A drought is a period when a region has less precipitation than normal. Drought can affect a fairly small area for a season or an entire continent for years. Too little rainfall can cause shortages in the water supply, destroy crops, and cause widespread famine. Drought also dries up topsoil, which then gets picked up by the wind and causes dust storms.

LOOK FOR: Periods of lower-than-normal rainfall, often accompanied by high temperatures. Use your rain gauge to compare your local rainfall with the normal amount expected for your area.

SEASON AND RANGE: Year-round; throughout North America.

CAUSES OF DROUGHT

Drought is caused by changes in large-scale weather patterns. In the United States drought is often associated with summer heat waves. Droughts are also caused by changes in ocean temperatures. El Niño—periods of warming waters in the equatorial Pacific Ocean—changes global weather patterns and brings droughts and flooding to many parts of the world.

WILDFIRES

Large areas of uncontrolled fires often accompany droughts. Usually ignited by lightning (but also sometimes by people), wildfires create huge amounts of smoke, which can darken the sky and reduce visibility.

131

AIR POLLUTION

Some air pollution occurs naturally, caused by particles in the air such as dust, ocean salt, ash from a nearby volcano, or pollen. But even natural air pollution can cause trouble. More than a million tons of pollen enter the air in North America each year, causing problems for people suffering from hay fever. Dust storms (like the one pictured) can greatly reduce visibility. Parched soil in drought-stricken areas is easily lifted into the air, forming swirling masses of dust. During the 1930s, drought across the central United States caused a large area to be called the Dust Bowl. During this bleak period, vast dust storms buried entire farmhouses!

LOOK FOR: Murky skies. High winds during a drought can mean that a dust storm is on the way.

SEASON AND RANGE: Year-round; throughout North America.

HAZE AND SMOG

Millions of tiny particles floating in the air can create haze, a yellowish or bluish veil against the sky. Cars, factories, power plants, and other things that burn fuel produce dense, gray or brown air pollution called smog. Smog usually reduces visibility and can cause eye and breathing problems. The photograph above shows smog over Los Angeles.

VOLCANIC ASH

Ash from erupting volcanoes can block sunlight and settle onto trees, plants, and cars. When it rains during a volcanic eruption, the ash falls like mud from the sky. Many other things can also affect how clear the air is, including sea spray, fog, and forest fires.

133

Ozone is a form of oxygen that is formed naturally in the atmosphere. In the upper atmosphere it is beneficial, but in the lower atmosphere, ozone is a harmful pollutant. It is formed through chemical reactions between automobile exhaust, industrial pollution, and sunlight. Many large cities, such as Los Angeles and Chicago, have unhealthy levels of ozone and smog.

INVERSIONS

Weather and air pollution go hand-in-hand. Los Angeles would not be so smoggy if it did not get so much sunlight, because sunlight is an important ingredient in the chemical reactions that form ozone and other air pollutants. Another weather condition, called temperature inversion, contributes to unhealthy pollution levels. During inversions the ground-level temperature is cooler than temperatures at higher altitudes. Inversions prevent the polluted, ground-level air from mixing with cleaner air at higher altitudes.

LIGHTNING POLLUTION

The intense heat of lightning bolts, over 50,000°F (27,000°C), splits apart gas molecules into individual nitrogen and oxygen atoms. The atoms then combine differently and form two types of pollution: nitric oxide and nitrogen dioxide. With nearly 10 million lightning flashes occurring on earth each day, over 30 million tons of pollution is created this way every year. This natural pollutant combines with man-made pollution to form ozone and haze.

LOOK FOR: Hazy polluted air, warm temperatures, and a lot of sunshine.

SEASON AND RANGE: Mainly summer; throughout North America, especially in warm urban areas.

135

ACID RAIN

Air pollution from automobiles and factories often travels long distances through the atmosphere—sometimes thousands of miles—before returning to earth in rain or snow. During its travel the pollution has many days to participate in chemical reactions. Sulfur dioxide and nitrogen oxides from automobile and industrial emissions mix with cloud water, changing into sulfuric and nitric acids. Far from their original source, these acids fall from the sky as acid rain and acid snow.

LOOK FOR: Crystal-clear lakes and streams. Acid rain can kill underwater plants and algae, making the water look strangely clear.

SEASON AND RANGE: Year-round; throughout North America.

DAMAGE TO NATURE

Acid rain is especially damaging to forests, lakes, and streams. The acids draw poisonous minerals out of soil that cause diseases in plants and animals.

DAMAGE TO BUILDINGS

Acid rain also damages structures such as buildings, bridges, and statues. Over many years these objects become pitted, decayed, and discolored.

137

In addition to puffy white clouds floating across a deep blue background, the sky presents many colorful displays. Sky colors are caused by the sun's visible light rays passing through air molecules and floating particles. The molecules and particles scatter, or change the direction of, the sunlight. Air molecules scatter blue light more than other colors, so when we look at the sky we usually see blue.

SEASON AND RANGE: Year-round; throughout North America.

SUNRISE AND SUNSET

Beautiful sunrise and sunset colors occur when the atmosphere is full of small particles. These particles can be sea spray, pollution, or dust churned up by an approaching storm.

SILVER LININGS

A bright sun shining through a cumulus congestus cloud creates a "silver lining" effect—a bright ring around a darker cloud. The beams of light are crepuscular rays—shafts of sunlight scattered by floating particles.

139

MIRAGES

Mirages happen when sunlight travels through air of different temperatures and bends or distorts images in the distance. During a mirage, objects appear to be distorted, wavy, upside down, or enlarged. The most fantastic type of atmospheric mirage, the Fata Morgana, causes distant everyday objects to resemble fabulous castles and waterfalls.

LOOK FOR: Images that appear watery, distorted, and displaced above or below their true location.

SEASON AND RANGE: Year-round; throughout North America, especially over hot pavement and over water. The Fata Morgana is sometimes seen over the Great Lakes.

INFERIOR MIRAGES

Inferior mirages cause distant objects to appear upside-down and below their actual location. This deceptive phenomenon occurs only when ground-level air is much warmer than the air above.

SUPERIOR MIRAGES

Superior mirages form when ground-level air is much colder than the air above. Distant objects appear to float above their actual location, sometimes upside-down.

141

AURORA BOREALIS

Auroras are shimmering nighttime displays of colored lights hundreds of miles above the earth's surface. Known as aurora borealis, or northern lights, in the Northern Hemisphere (and as aurora australis, or southern lights, in the Southern Hemisphere), they sometimes appear as eerie cascades of flickering colors. Other times auroras look like curtains, bands, or waves of colored light.

LOOK FOR: Arcs, bands, rays, or large curtains of light that seem to dance or flicker in a clear night sky. Colors may range from pale green to combinations of red, green, yellow, and violet.

SEASON AND RANGE: Year-round; most common in areas close to the north and south poles, but have been seen in North America as far south as southern U.S.

HOW AURORAS FORM

Auroras are caused by disturbances on the sun's surface that send electrically charged particles hurtling into space. The particles smash into the upper levels of the atmosphere, causing them to glow in various colors.

AURORAS IN SPACE

Occurring between 50 and 120 miles

Halos appear as large rings of light around the sun or moon. They form when sunlight passes through the millions of ice crystals in a cirrostratus cloud. Halos are mostly white with a faint red color on the inner edge and faint blue on the outer edge. Cirrostratus clouds pass overhead several hours before an approaching warm front, so a halo is often a good clue that rain or snow is on the way.

LOOK FOR: A ring or part of a ring around the sun or moon. Always use your hand to block out the sun before you look.

SEASON AND RANGE: Year-round; throughout North America.

SUNDOGS

Sundogs are bright spots of rainbow-colored light that, like halos, form when sunlight passes through cirrostratus cloud crystals. They are often seen on the sides of halos, but can also be found without a halo.

SUN PILLARS

Sun pillars are columns of light extending above or below the sun. They are caused by sunlight reflecting off of ice crystals and can be seen when the sun is low in the sky, either rising or setting.

RAINBOWS

Rainbows, one of the most common but most spectacular sky displays, are caused by the reflection and refraction (bending) of sunlight passing through raindrops. In heavy rains a double rainbow can often be seen.

LOOK FOR: Rainbows can be seen only when it is raining, the sun is low in the sky and shining brightly, and you are standing between the sun and the rain. You are most likely to see one in the late afternoon or early morning. Turn your back to the sun and watch the sky to see if a rainbow forms.

SEASON AND RANGE: Spring, summer, and fall; throughout North America.

CORONAS

A corona is a small circle of colored light caused by water droplet clouds. Much smaller than a halo, a corona forms a small disk around the sun or moon (corona means "crown" in Latin).

IRIDESCENCE

Beautiful patches of color in clouds near the sun or moon are called iridescence. Similar to a corona, iridescence is caused by sunlight passing through water droplet clouds.

147

GREEN FLASH

Very rarely when the sun is setting over the sea a brief flash of bright green light can be seen. The green flash is most often spotted when the air is clear of clouds and haze. Occurring a split second after the sun sets, it appears at the top of the ball of the sun or sometimes just above it. Air molecules in the atmosphere scatter the final rays of sunlight to produce this short-lived phenomenon.

LOOK FOR: A flash of green light just as the sun drops below the horizon. Best seen from a beach or out at sea.

SEASON AND RANGE: Year-round; mainly over ocean areas that are free of air pollution.

VOLCANIC TWILIGHT

Twilight is both the time after sunset when the sky is not yet dark and the time before sunrise when the sky begins getting light. The sky at twilight is normally shades of blue, yellow, and green (pictured above). When a volcano has erupted somewhere on earth, a vast quantity of particles can be spewed into the air around the entire globe. The volcanic ash particles in the atmosphere can turn the sky spectacular colors at twilight, often red, orange, and purple (pictured below).

Sunset, Joshua Tree National Monument

How to use the reference section

The **Glossary,** which begins below, contains words used by meteorologists and naturalists when they talk about weather. If you run across a word in this book that you do not understand, check the glossary for a definition. Also in this section is a listing of **Resources,** including books, videotapes, CDs, Web sites, and organizations devoted to North American weather. Finally, there is an **Index** of all the types of weather covered in the Field Guide section of this book.

GLOSSARY

Acid rain
Precipitation that contains sulfuric and nitric acids, caused by pollution from cars and factories.

Air mass
A large body of air with distinct levels of temperature and humidity.

Air pressure
The weight of the air pressing down on the earth.

Altitude
The distance of an object above the surface of a planet, as in an airplane's distance from the earth.

Anemometer
A weather instrument that measures wind speed.

Anticyclone
A high-pressure system.

Anvil
The term used to describe the flattened top of a thunderstorm cloud.

Atmosphere
The layers of air that surround the earth. The bottom layer is the troposphere, where most of the earth's weather occurs.

Barometer
A weather instrument that measures air pressure. A drop in the barometer indicates the approach of a low-pressure system.

Climate
The average weather in a certain place or during a certain season.

Clouds
Floating collections of water droplets or ice crystals. Different cloud types form in different weather conditions and provide important forecasting clues.

Cold front
The boundary created when a cold air mass collides with a warm air mass.

Condensation
The process by which water vapor (a gas) converts to liquid water, which is how most clouds form. In below-freezing temperatures, water vapor may convert directly to solid water (ice).

Condensation nuclei
The tiny particles in the air around which cloud droplets form.

Convection
The process by which warm air rises and cools, often condensing to form puffy cumulus clouds.

Coriolis force
The force that causes Northern Hemisphere winds to curve to the right and Southern Hemisphere winds to curve to the left.

Cyclone
A low-pressure system.

Dew point
The temperature at which condensation occurs. The dew point temperature varies according to the amount of moisture in the air.

Doppler radar
An advanced kind of radar that measures wind speed and locates areas of precipitation.

Downdraft
The downward movement of cool air, often inside a thunderstorm cloud.

Electromagnetic radiation
Energy generated from both the sun and the earth, including sunlight, heat energy, and harmful ultraviolet rays.

Evacuate
To leave an area, usually to escape danger.

Evaporation
The process of liquid water converting to water vapor.

Front
The boundary between two air masses. The several types of fronts bring distinct weather patterns.

Funnel cloud
A spinning cone-shaped cloud that drops out of a severe thunderstorm cloud.

Greenhouse effect
The recycling of the sun's energy by the atmosphere. Like the roof on a greenhouse, the atmosphere lets energy in but keeps some from escaping.

Gust front
An area of shifting winds beneath a downdraft in a thunderstorm cloud.

Halo
A ring of light around the sun or moon caused by sunlight passing through ice crystals in cirrostratus clouds.

Lenticular clouds page 79

Hemisphere
The top and bottom halves of the earth are called the Northern and Southern Hemispheres.

High-pressure system
A large mass of air that spins in a clockwise direction in the Northern Hemisphere (counter-clockwise in the Southern Hemisphere) and usually brings fair weather.

GLOSSARY

Double rainbow page 146

Horizon
The line where the earth and sky seem to meet when you look into the distance.

Humidity
The amount of water vapor in the air. When there is a lot of vapor, the air is called humid.

Hurricane
A tropical storm with destructive spinning winds over 74 miles (119 km) per hour.

Hygrometer
A weather instrument that measures humidity.

Iridescence
Colorful patches in clouds caused by sunlight passing through the water droplets.

Jet stream
Fast-moving currents of air high in the atmosphere.

Latent heat
Heat released into the air when water vapor condenses and forms clouds.

Low-pressure system
A large mass of air that spins in a counterclockwise direction in the Northern Hemisphere (clockwise in the Southern Hemisphere) and usually brings precipitation.

Mesocyclone
An area of spinning winds that occurs inside a severe thunderstorm cloud.

Meteorologist
A scientist who studies and predicts the weather.

Occluded front
The boundary formed when a cold front collides with a warm front.

Ozone layer
A layer high in the atmosphere that filters out most of the sun's dangerous ultraviolet rays.

Precipitation
Any kind of water falling from the sky, such as rain, drizzle, snow, hail, or freezing rain.

Pressure gradient force
The force that causes air to move from areas of high pressure toward areas of low pressure.

Radar
A weather instrument that sends out radio waves that bounce off water droplets and ice crystals.

Radiosonde
A miniature weather instrument carried by a gas-filled balloon. It supplies information about weather from ground level to the upper atmosphere.

Rain gauge
A weather instrument that measures rainfall.

Relative humidity
The percentage of water vapor that the air can hold at a given time. A relative humidity of 90 percent means that the air is nearly full of water vapor and may soon become saturated, or unable to hold additional water vapor.

Satellite
A weather instrument that orbits the earth, taking photographs and collecting measurements of the upper atmosphere.

Solar radiation
Electromagnetic radiation (energy) coming from the sun, including sunlight, ultraviolet, and infrared radiation.

Squall
A sudden gusty wind, often accompanied by precipitation.

Stationary front
The boundary of cold and warm air masses moving side by side.

Supercooled water droplets
Water droplets that remain liquid below freezing temperatures.

Temperature
The amount of heat the air is holding.

Thermometer
A weather instrument that measures air temperature.

Tornado
A funnel cloud with destructive spinning winds that drops from a severe thunderstorm cloud and touches the ground.

Tropical storm
A storm that forms over warm waters, with spinning winds between 40 and 73 miles (65–117 km) per hour.

Turbulence
Irregular movements of the wind, such as gusts and lulls.

Updraft
The upward movement of warm air. Updrafts can be found beneath and inside all types of cumulus clouds.

Velocity
The term used to describe wind speed.

Visibility
The farthest distance it is possible to see at any particular time.

Vortex
A spinning mass of air and clouds.

Warm front
The boundary created when a warm air mass collides with a cold air mass.

Water cycle
The cyclical movement of water from the earth to the air and back again.

Water vapor
Water in its invisible gas form.

Weather
The condition of the air at a particular time and place.

Wind
The sideways movement of air.

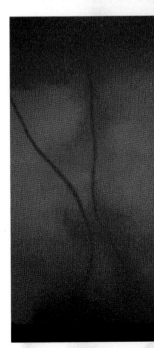

Tornadoes page 102

RESOURCES

FOR FURTHER READING

Can It Really Rain Frogs? The World's Strangest Weather Events
Spencer Christian and Antonia Felix
John Wiley & Sons, 1997

Dangerous Natural Phenomena
(Encyclopedia of Danger Series)
Missy Allen and Michel Peissel
Chelsea House Publishers, 1993

Eye of the Storm: Chasing Storms with Warren Faidley
Stephen Kramer
Putnam Publishing Group, 1997

Frost: Causes and Effects
(Weather Watch Series)
Philip Steele
Franklin Watts, Inc., 1991

Hands on Meteorology
Zbigniew Sorbjan
American Meteorological Society, 1996

Hazy Skies: Weather and the Environment
(How's the Weather? Series)
Jonathan D. W. Kahl
Lerner Publications, 1997

Heatwave: Causes and Effects
(Weather Watch Series)
Philip Steele
Franklin Watts, Inc., 1991

Hurricanes
(First Book Series)
Sally Lee
Franklin Watts, Inc., 1994

Looking at Weather
(David Suzuki's Looking At Series)
David Suzuki and Barbara Hehner
John Wiley & Sons, 1991

National Audubon Society Field Guide to North American Weather
David M. Ludlum
Alfred A. Knopf, 1991

National Audubon Society Pocket Guide to Clouds and Storms
David M. Ludlum, Ronald L. Holle, and Richard A. Keen
Alfred A. Knopf, 1995

Rain: Causes and Effects
(Weather Watch Series)
Philip Steele
Franklin Watts, Inc., 1991

Simple Weather Experiments with Everyday Materials
Muriel Mandell
Sterling Publications, 1991

The Sky Above Us
(Around and About Series)
Kate Petty and Jakki Wood
Barrons, 1993

Sky and Weather
(Project Science Series)
Alan Ward
Franklin Watts, Inc., 1993

Storm Warning: Tornadoes and Hurricanes
(How's the Weather? Series)
Jonathan D. W. Kahl
Lerner Publications, 1993

Super Science Book of Weather
Kay Davies
Thomson Learning, 1993

Thunderbolt: Learning About Lightning
(How's the Weather? Series)
Jonathan D. W. Kahl
Lerner Publications, 1993

Usborne Book of Weather Facts
Anita Ganeri
E D C Publications, 1987

Thunderstorm page 126

Weather
(Learn About Series)
Robin Kerrod and J. W. Wright
Lorenz Books, 1997

Weather
(Scholastic Discovery Box Series)
Scholastic, Inc., 1997

Weather
(Spotter's Guide Series)
Francis Wilson and Felicity
Mansfield
E D C Publications, 1995

**Weather Explained: A Beginner's
Guide to the Elements**
(Your World Explained Series)
Derek M. Elsom
Henry Holt & Co., 1997

**Weather Forecaster (Be an
Expert)**
Barbara Taylor-Cork
Orchard Books, 1992

The Weather Sky
Bruce McMillan
Farrar, Straus & Giroux, 1991

The Weather Tracker's Kit
(Explore the Changing Forces of
Nature Series)
Gregory C. Aaron
Running Press, 1991

**Weather Watch: Forecasting the
Weather**
(How's the Weather? Series)
Jonathan D. W. Kahl
Lerner Publications, 1996

**Wind and Weather: Climates,
Clouds, Snow, Tornados, and
How Weather Is Predicted**
(Scholastic Voyages of Discovery
Series)
Liane Onish (Editor)
Scholastic Inc., 1995

TAPES AND DISKS

Cyclone
(National Geographic Videos)
Columbia Tristar Home Video,
1995

Tornado Video Classic Series
The Tornado Project
Tel: 802-748-2505

**The Weather Tracker's Kit:
Explore the Changing
Forces of Nature**
(Interactive CD-ROM)
Gregory C. Aaron
Running Press, 1995

Wonders of Weather Series
(The Learning Channel Videos)
KingWorld Direct

ORGANIZATIONS

American Meteorological Society
45 Beacon Street
Boston, MA 02108-3693
http://www.ametsoc.org

EarthWatch International
680 Mount Auburn Street
P.O. Box 403
Watertown, MA 02272
Tel: 612-476-9005
http://www.earthwatch.org

National Audubon Society
700 Broadway
New York, NY 10003-9562
Tel: 212-979-3000
http://www.audubon.org

Sierra Club
85 2nd Street, 2nd Floor
San Francisco, CA 94105-3441
Tel: 415-977-5500
http://www.sierraclub.org

*Hurricane Erin, Florida,
August 2, 1995*

WEB SITES

The Atomic Moose:
http://www.datasync.com/
~moose/ atmosphere.html

Audubon Web site for Kids:
http://www.audubon.org/kid/
index.html

**Center for Analysis and
Prediction of Storms:**
http://www.caps.uoknor.edu

**Center for Ocean-Land-
Atmosphere Studies:**
http: //grads.iges.org/cola.html

Dan's Wild Wild Weather Page:
http://whnt19.com/kidwx/

**EarthWatch—Weather on
Demand:**
http://www.earthwatch.com

Virtual Weather Map Room:
http://www.uwm.edu/~kahl/106/
106_wx.html

Weather Dude:
http://www.nwlink.com/~wxdude

INDEX

Page numbers in **bold** point to the subject's page in the field guide.

Ice crystals on window

PHOTO/ILLUSTRATION CREDITS

159

Prepared and produced by
Chanticleer Press, Inc.

Publisher: Andrew Stewart
Founder: Paul Steiner

Chanticleer Staff:
Editor-in-Chief: Amy K. Hughes
Editor: Miriam Harris
Assistant Editor: Michelle Bredeson
Editorial Assistants: Kate Jacobs, Tessa Kale
Photo Director: Zan Carter
Photo Traffic Coordinator: Jennifer McClanaghan
Rights and Permissions Manager: Alyssa Sachar
Art Director: Drew Stevens
Designer: Vincent Mejia
Assistant Designer: Anthony Liptak
Director of Production: Alicia Mills
Production Assistant: Philip Pfeifer
Publishing Assistant: Karin Murphy

Contributors:
Writer: Jonathan D. W. Kahl
Consultants: Mark Serreze and Rick Cech
Paintings: Howard S. Friedman
Maps and Diagrams: Ortelius Design
Icons: Holly Kowitt
Photo Editor: Yvonne Silver, Artemis Picture Research Group, Inc.
Editors: Pamela Nelson, Holly Thompson

Scholastic, Inc., Staff:
Editorial Director: Wendy Barish, Creative Director: David Saylor,
Managing Editor: Manuela Soares, Manufacturing Manager: Janet Castiglione

Original Series Design: Chic Simple Design